Ten Years of
The Asian Writer

Edited by Farhana Shaikh

First published 2018 by Dahlia Publishing Ltd
6 Samphire Close Hamilton
Leicester LE5 1RW
ISBN 9780995634480

Printed and bound by Grosvenor Group

CONTENTS

FOREWORD
Farhana Shaikh

I set up *The Asian Writer* to raise the profile of published authors and provide a platform to showcase new and emerging voices of British Asian literature. As a young writer, at the time, I was fed up by the lack of visibility of those writers who had defied the odds to be published and I wondered why their stories were still missing from the mainstream.

The Asian Writer was borne out of a selfish need and curiosity I had about writers who had done exactly what I had wanted to do: finish a book and get it published. I was hungry for their stories, and wondered whether their lives had been anything like my own. I also wanted to find my tribe, a community of like-minded individuals, who had perhaps like me, ignored their parent's wishes to pursue a career in banking, to put pen to paper.

It's been more than a decade since *The Asian Writer's* first interviews appeared online and while the publication has seen many changes in terms of look and design, its spirit remains the same today. It's with the same dogged determination that I seek to find new and emerging voices and share their stories of success, but also their stories of struggle.

And trying to keep going as a writer in the current climate is all too often about struggle. The struggle to tell our stories as we wish, the struggle to unlearn some of the things that we are handed down, and the struggle to get published. But if we are to make it as writers, we must keep going, we must have confidence to tell our stories, not the ones we think will be published or those which we think other people want to hear, but those that make us laugh, and cry, and expose that vulnerability in us, as we write. We must write freely and without the weight of expectation.

Author interviews have always been a big part of *The Asian Writer*. It's through the author's own voice and words that there is often so much to learn about what it takes to be a writer. The Asian Writer has profiled more than 150 writers since those first four interviews – with Mohsin Hamid, Roopa Farooki, Imran Ahmad and Priya Basil – appeared online. And it gives me great pleasure to reprint those as part of this collection, alongside some of my favourite interviews over the years.

It's not the first time we have ventured into print. In 2010, we published our first collection, *Happy Birthday to Me*, which featured emerging voices such as Niven Govinden and Shamshad Khan, alongside new voices at the time, such as Nikesh Shukla and Farhana Khalique. That year, also marked a change of focus for me, as I set up a small press, Dahlia Publishing in a bid to publish writers who were, and still are, largely ignored by the mainstream. The publishing press has allowed me to take risks in championing new forms other than the novel.

Since 2012, it's been thrilling to recognise and reward the best emerging talents through *The Asian Writer* Short Story Prize. The competition has produced a sublime list of winners and shortlisted writers, some of whom have gone on to find mainstream success, and others who continue to persevere. It's a real honour to showcase the writing of our first prize winners, which goes some way to highlight the range and breadth of ideas that new writers are often concerned with. Work that is often brave, unexpected, and delightful.

And it's in this space of working with new writers, that I've found myself at home. For the past three years, I've been running *The Asian Writer's* Becoming a Writer course. It has been a real honour to work with so many South Asian women, from all over the world, and to provide a supportive and nurturing environment where creativity and ideas can flourish and we can begin to unravel and overcome the barriers necessary to be able to sit down and write. And that is what we must all do if we are to succeed in completing the thing that we set out to do. We must show up at the page. We must give in to our artist. We must sit down and write.

Since 2015, there has been renewed efforts by the industry to tackle the lack of diversity and representation that continues to prevail and we no longer find ourselves in the space we once did. Things are shifting. However, *The Asian Writer's* work is far from over. And so we must continue to profile the excellent work of published writers, we must provide opportunities for new and emerging writers to showcase their work and we must continue to take care of ourselves, our work and one another.

I hope you enjoy reading this collection which hopes to shine a spotlight on what we've achieved together over a period of ten years, as well as showcase the incredible talent of new and emerging voices of British Asian literature.

VASEEM KHAN

This speech was made at The Asian Writer Festival at The Wesley on October 20th 2018.

First of all, let me thank Farhana for inviting me here today and for her continuing efforts in tirelessly promoting her corner of the publishing world.

The title of my talk is 'Call me a writer', and what I mean by that is all of us, whether we are at the beginning of our writer journeys or not, whether we write purely for pleasure or something more, are connected by one overwhelming desire – to set down in words the ideas that we are constantly being assaulted by. They come at us in the middle of the night, while walking along the street, as we are replying to the latest tedious email at work. Ideas that seem to parachute through the cosmos with the sole intention of landing inside our brains and setting off explosive chain reactions that compel us to put everything else aside and retreat into bubbles of fictional reality that we have the privilege of creating. That is when we are most alive. That is why we write and why we call ourselves writers.

But let me begin by winding back the clock. We're going back in time to 1997 and a bright-eyed young man is getting off the plane at Bombay International Airport (as it was then called). Take a look at him. He is 23 years old, born and raised in East London, and although he has come to India to work as a management consultant, he firmly believes that one day he is going to be a writer, rich, successful, the toast of the literary fraternity. At that stage his balloon has not been burst by repeated rejections or the realities of the publishing industry. But we'll come to that in a moment.

On that day I walked out into a wall of searing 40 degree heat, jumped in a cab and found myself, ten minutes later, at a set of traffic lights. There was a terrific thumping on the side of the taxi and I turned to find a large man dressed in a wonderful midnight blue sari, my first encounter with a eunuch. A trifle disconcerted, I focused my gaze on the main road, and a great river of passing traffic: honking rickshaws, hooting trucks, bikes, cows, goats, dogs, and a chattering stream of humanity in fifty shades of brown. That's when I saw the most surreal sight of all, for, lumbering through this chaos came an enormous grey Indian elephant with a mahout on its back, a sight that has stayed with me ever since.

This then was the genesis of the idea that eventually sold my series, the introduction of an elephant into a crime novel. It was ten years later, when I returned to the UK, that I actually made the decision to put all of those wonderful memories of India into a novel, together with that symbolic elephant. That first book, *The Unexpected Inheritance of Inspector Chopra*, became a Times bestseller and set the foundation for the series, the fifth of which comes out next year. My aim with these books is to showcase the real India that I experienced, not the mythologised version of India that western depictions of the subcontinent often show us.

Over the past few years I have ticked pretty much every box I dreamed of as a young writer. Sales success, critical acclaim, literary awards, foreign translations, media exposure, talks up and down the country, and membership of a fraternity of fellow authors and book lovers. But the road to that (relative) success was long and hard, and, I hope, can provide insight for others such as yourselves who are at various stages of your own writer journeys.

I began in a home where reading was never a priority. My father couldn't read and didn't believe in books. My mother was literate but was too busy raising kids. It wasn't until I discovered the library system in my teenage years that the literary horizons opened up for me, and I began to realise that reading for pleasure – and constructing my own stories – was something that ignited a passion in me unrivalled by anything else I could or would ever do. It was also through the libraries that I first encountered Terry Pratchett's fantastic Discworld series of comic fantasy novels. As I read these wonderful books, and marvelled at the effortless manner in which they seemed to be constructed, it occurred to me that this whole writing business seemed really easy – it was only later that I could appreciate that Pratchett made it *look* easy. I resolved there and then to become a novelist and wrote my first novel aged seventeen, a means of avoiding having to go to university and, ultimately, get a real job.

There was, of course, one small problem with this cunning plan. That first book was *awful*. And that is the first lesson I have for you. As young or novice authors it is difficult to have enough distance from your work to be objective. Which why it is so important to have others around you to bounce ideas off, to help you hone your craft, to bolster your confidence when those rejection letters tumble through your letterbox and detonate like little grenades inside your soul. As a young writer it can be difficult to find a like-minded fraternity – which is why initiatives such as The Asian Writer are so important. I myself spent twenty-four years trying to get published and never once did I show another human soul anything I had written. This was a mistake and I urge you not to repeat it.

After my first book was rejected I went back to the drawing board. I eventually wrote six more novels over the course of those twenty-four years until I received a four-book deal from Hodder for the Chopra series. With each subsequent rejection during that soul-sapping period, I lost a little more of the Olympian confidence I had set out with as a young man. I began to question myself, my writing. I made the classic mistake of trying to follow the market. I wrote a literary novel, I wrote SF, I wrote thrillers. I would have gladly written a Gilbert and Sullivan style opera if I had thought it would get me published. At one point I had collected enough rejection letters to all but bury myself, both literally and figuratively. How did I manage to keep going? To keep churning out book after rejected book? The answer is simple. You do it because you love doing it, because writing lies at the very core of what makes you tick. That long journey – and the years since being published – have left me wiser and I hope I can pass on some of that wisdom today. So, for the second half of this talk I am going to set out for you the Five Commandments of Khan, my guide on how to make the best of your writing endeavours.

Commandant #1 - Put the cart before the horse.

As a younger writer you may well suffer from doubt. Believe me, even those of us with multiple books under our belt are sometimes stricken by such angst. Even as we furiously hack away on our laptops, working on the book which will finally see us achieve our goals – whether that be to simply construct a few beautiful lines of prose for our own sense of accomplishment or to write a national bestseller – we are wracked by imposter syndrome. You *must* overcome this.

One of the world's most famous literary novelists, John Irving, went through a similar crisis of confidence before he became an international bestseller. It got to the point where he debated with himself whether to continue writing or not. Things changed for him one day when he met an author he admired and explained his predicament. The writer in question gave him a wonderful piece of advice which I now bequeath to you. He told him: stop saying to yourself that you will *become* a writer. Tell yourself that you *are* a writer. This is what I mean by putting the cart before the horse. Admit to yourself that you are a writer, regardless of where your destination might lie. Commit to the course and enjoy the journey.

Commandant #2 - Put in the hard yards.

There is no substitute for learning your craft. It is the rare individual who is blessed with unadulterated natural talent. But even the Roger Federers' of this world have to put in thousands of hours of practise before they can release that potential. Young writers often labour under the false belief that pure talent is what makes a writer, as if literary genius is some sort of rare ability that only the lucky few are born with while the rest of us look enviously on with our faces pressed against the glass. Nothing could be further from the truth. There is no literary gene. Yes, some writers discover that it comes easier than others, but for most of us it is about *learning* how to write good prose, about developing a feel for language and dialogue, about learning how to construct a plot and avoid exposition. The only way to do this is by writing every day, and when you're not writing be editing, and when you're not editing be reading. It took me seven novels and two decades to get published. That may not be everyone's goal, but it was certainly mine. At the beginning of that period my writing was unpublishable, to put it kindly. By the end, I was writing well enough to be published – at that point I needed a slice of good fortune i.e. my latest offering landing on the desk of the right agent at the right time.

Commandant #3 - Put diversity into perspective.

The word diversity, as currently used in the publishing industry, has multiple meanings. To some it means bringing along writers of colour to correct underrepresentation. To others it means a gradual evolution of the type of people who work behind the scenes in the industry - agents, editors, publicists. And to others it means publishing stories about people from these underrepresented communities, not necessarily written by writers from those same backgrounds. We all know there are invisible barriers, some systemic, that have made it difficult for writers of colour to break into the industry. I myself wondered for years if that was the real reason I was always the bridesmaid and never the bride. I am delighted that now publishers at least appear to be attempting to tackle the problem. But my advice for you, as individuals, is this: the best thing you can do is put the diversity issue to one side. Dwelling too long on whether you are being hard done by because of 'diversity' can sap you of vital energy. I am not suggesting that you not acknowledge the issue or indeed not get involved in helping turn the tide. But compartmentalise such feelings, so that it doesn't rob you of the creative vigour you need to continue to grow as a writer. *Ask not what the publishing industry can do for you, but what you can do for the industry.* I know that's difficult. I recently proposed a new series to my publisher featuring a white, Scottish dwarf as the lead protagonist. I was politely told that this might not work for me. I interpret this as meaning that I am neither white, nor Scottish, nor a dwarf and thus not entitled to write this sort of book. But the writer in me rejects this. I could easily waste a lot of time butting heads with my agent and publisher arguing my case. Instead, I choose to move on, write the next thing that inspires me, leaving such battles for another day. It is still my intention to see some of these books published, but I've realised that playing the long game will work more to my advantage. I urge you to think about a *career* in writing, and not just a single book. If your goal is to be published remember that being published should just be the start of your journey, not the end. And if your goal is simply to use writing as a way of expressing the creative side of your personality, then again, think of it as a lifelong endeavour of learning and improvement.

Commandant #4 - Put your commercial hat on.

For those of you keen on seeing your work in print, it is important to realise that the mainstream publishing industry is now a very commercial place. When a commissioning editor wishes to buy a book they must present a business case before they can get sign off. That case must articulate who the audience is for your book, what marketing hooks can be used to sell it, which bestselling authors it can be compared to. These are the things you need to be thinking about when writing, and particularly when prepping your submission. For instance, in my case, the Baby Ganesh

Detective Agency series was bought by Hodder because it worked on multiple levels – as crime novels, as explorations of modern India, as a set of intriguing characters that readers would wish to revisit, including that unique hook of a baby elephant. You must ask yourself whether your books can also work on multiple levels. Why? Because this convinces publishers that they can sell your book to a wider audience.

On the subject of submissions: my agent receives four thousand submissions a year. He cannot read them all so he tends to read the first five pages and if the story hasn't grabbed him by then he doesn't read the rest. Your challenge is to make your opening *sensational*. I received a four-book deal from Hodder practically for the opening chapter of *The Unexpected Inheritance of Inspector Chopra*. And if you want to know why you will have to read the book. Which brings me to the other important skill that authors must now demonstrate to get publishers onside – the ability to sell yourself and your work. For instance: every writer must have, in his or her arsenal, a fifteen-minute pitch talk about themselves and their book which is lively and engaging and which they can deliver flawlessly. These commercial imperatives cannot be ignored if your goal is to become a published author hoping for a stable career.

Commandant #5 - Put your identity front and centre.

People talk about discovering your voice as an author – it's actually more akin to discovering your identity. Authors are like superheroes. Most of us have those pesky day jobs, but, once we get behind a laptop, we shed our work clothes to reveal our superhero costumes. But what kind of superhero are you? Are you a young adult author? Are you an angst-filled literary novelist? Are you a writer of dark psychological thrillers, the new Gillian Flynn? Are you someone who writes soul-searching poetry for nothing more than your own pleasure? We all have different identities, different heritages and if you use that in your writing – as I do in my books – then fantastic, do it and be the best writer you can be. But never make the mistake of believing or allowing others to believe that that is all you are. Some of you may know an author called Bali Rai. He writes young adult fiction, and has over forty books to his credit. He was recently asked in an interview: "What are the challenges of becoming an author and being a British Asian?" His reply was quite telling. He said that the biggest challenge had been trying to break free of the pigeonhole that he had been placed in. He had been labelled as a British Asian author and that labelling (and I quote) had become a "noose around my neck". As a brown man, he is expected to write about other brown people. This can be to your advantage, and if that's what you wish to do then good luck to you. I am a brown man who writes about a brown protagonist and I have had great success doing it. But remember that first and foremost you are a writer, and a writer, by definition, has the world as his or her canvas. In the end, you have to write something that *you* believe in, even if no one else does. Yet. Your writing identity must define your work, not the other way around.

I'll finish by wishing you all the very best in your careers. And remember, as of this moment you are no longer trying to become writers. You *are* writers. So, if anyone asks, tell them to call you a writer.

Vaseem Khan first saw an elephant lumbering down the middle of the road in 1997 when he arrived in India to work as a management consultant. It was the most unusual thing he had ever encountered and served as the inspiration behind his series of crime novels. He returned to the UK in 2006 and now works at University College London for the Department of Security and Crime Science where he is astonished on a daily basis by the way modern science is being employed to tackle crime. Elephants are third on his list of passions, first and second being great literature and cricket, not always in that order.

ROOPA FAROOKI

This speech was made at The Asian Writer Festival at the Royal Asiatic Society on October 21st 2017.

What an honour to be asked to speak here, at the inaugural Asian writer festival. Celebrating ten years of celebrating work by Asian writers, a true testament to Farhana's spirit and tenacity.

And that will be the theme of this talk. Spirit. The passion for what we do. And tenacity, the motivation to keep doing it. What we do, and why it's important.

Ten years ago, I was publishing my first novel. I was completely unknown, what they call in the trade a slush pile author. It sounds like a derogatory phrase, but it's just fact; my manuscript was in a pile with all the other hopeful submissions from unknowns. I probably seemed a bit of a dilettante, with my background in corporate finance and advertising. Doing campaigns for Harpic with catchy little lines, like what does your loo say about you. The truth was that I'd been writing since I was seven years old. It wasn't a hobby. Sometimes it wasn't even a pleasure. I wrote then for the same reason I write now. Because I must. Because there is nothing else that I would want to do.

But who would know that? Who would know the intense passion, the intent, with which I wrote, unless I sat them down across a table, and made it known. Unless I spoke out. I didn't have the opportunity to do that when I was first published, I was living in another country with two babies less than 2 years old. And as a result, in those early days, I had some pretty politically incorrect comments about my books, based not on the words I wrote, but the smiley press photo my publisher took of me, and the pretty paisley endpapers. "So, do you write Chicken Tikka Lit, then?" With a comment, muttered under the breath, "I'm so tired of Attractive Asian authors churning out this sort of book." But not so muttered, nor under the breath, as it still made it into the published review.

So this is what we're up against. And let's not pretend for a moment that it's a level playing field. Of course, everyone in the arts fights to be recognised for what we do. I acknowledge that. We feel obliged to justify the importance of what we do, even, to explain why unwinding our narratives from ourselves, spinning stories from the stuff which makes us, has a value. It's frustrating, as scientists don't have the same obligation to justify their daily work, at least not in the field of medicine, where I am currently training. Doctors may help us stay fitter for longer, but what are we being kept fitter for? For a better understanding of our daily struggle, the search for that thing that gets us up in the morning, the resolution of that thing that keeps us awake in the night. The discovery of passion, unburdening of fear.

So yes. All artists fight for the right to practice their craft, and we, as Asian writers, fight more than most. We fight for our places on publisher's lists, for our places on the prize lists, for our places in the promotions. We writers, both men and women, may be dismissed because of our appearance, because of the boxes we have been put in, the brands that publishers have built. Accused of being too political, or not political enough. Too Asian, or not enough.

In short, we may be judged for something other than our words.

We can and should be relentless in telling our stories, and some may hear, but they may not listen, and then our stories are only half told, not reaching our readers, dripping away like tears in the rain and drops in the ocean. I always tell my students in Oxford that writing involves a triangle of relationships, between author and character and reader. We need to reach our readers, we need to try.

So ten years ago, The Asian Writer, a newbie like me, took my work seriously. And I wasn't afraid to take my work seriously. Which I think is an important lesson for all new writers. Writing the story is important, but speak out loud, make a noise. And all our voices together are powerful. A storm. A flood.

If you don't treat your work with respect, who else will? If you don't tirelessly promote your place on the programme, who will? It's worth remembering that no one cares more for the wellbeing of your work, than you. And that passion is infectious. Find advocates. Celebrate them. When my first editor fell in love with my first novel, the sales team said that she brought it to them and her eyes were shining. And that was worth more than all the box ticking in the world.

And what of the work itself? There are many books and courses teaching you how to write, and if that sounds somewhat oxymoronic, for something that is creative rather than interpretive, artistic more than artisan, at least you can be taught to write better.

But what you choose to write, or rather what chooses you, that spark and passion that takes you through the 90 thousand words of your novel, that's unique to you. It sounds rather obvious, but there's a lot of work, a lot of typing, that goes into a book. Lots of blank pages to fill in a lonely room. There's your blood on the keyboard, your sweat and tears. There's doubt and compromise, as you leave your imaginary world to earn your living, to do the school run, to care for parent or child or spouse or friend, to pay your debts and your dues, to present a sane and civilised face to the world.

I firmly believe that good writing has a cost to the writer, it takes something from you, so when you put it on the page, you can be sure that it is something of value. It has been carved from the closest place to your heart that you can spare.

And that is why you cannot write with insincerity. You cannot write something that you think other people want to read, if it is not what you want to write. Following the market is like panning for fool's gold, because maybe you can fool someone long enough for an elevator pitch or even yourself for a few chapters, but you cannot write if you do not care. And this is where it gets tricky, because we may find a publisher who expects us to write a certain kind of story. Or who tells us not to write a certain kind of story.

And I am going to urge you now, write what you will. Dance as though no one is watching. Because the truth is that no one will guarantee you a readership, for each story you write. No agent, editor or publisher. But that's ok. If you write with passion, if you write the story that only you can tell, and you do the best with whatever talent you possess, you know that you have done all that you can do as an artist and practitioner. And if that story does not find an audience, for whatever reason, there are always more stories to tell. They are spinning around you, flowing through you, from you, and you just have to reach out, and pluck your next story from the air. And make it real.

And we are Asian writers. We are here because of a common background or interest, we may be first or second or third generation, we may have Asian spouses or siblings or children, we may write about the place we fell in love with or where we made our homes. We are those who left, those who stayed, and those who discovered. We have wings and we have roots. All of these stories are important. I would never tell another writer what to write, but I made a decision to people my novels with people like me, like my parents, like my Anglo Asian children. Because if I do not put moderate Muslims at the heart of my literary fiction, I do not know who else will. And I made a decision not to write about cultural difference or cultural clash, I write about people. Flawed and fragile, knotted into their worlds by their relationships, tossed about by the turbulent emotions.

A book is an invitation. It opens up your imaginary world, the place at the heart of you, and you ask people to come in, to walk around in your world, to try on your shoes. To understand what is under your skin. We are divided in despicable ways, we have burning bridges between us. So write your story and invite everyone in.

And the more we do that, in these increasingly troubled times, the more we explore what we share rather than what divides us, the more we encourage empathy while understanding otherness, then we do not simply justify our craft. We are redeemed by it.

But let's talk about tenacity. It's all very well to talk about the stories that are written with passion, but what keeps you going, when your stories are rejected. Let's debunk the myth. Because for every writer with a stonking six figure debut fresh from the Faber academy, smiling toothily out of the newspapers with ironic self-awareness, there are writers who have written book after book before getting published, let alone getting their big breakthrough. Most writers I know have had at least two books rejected, before their debut novel. I'm one of them.

I don't think we talk about failure enough. I don't think we normalise it. Because failing to publish your work, isn't a failure. It's apprenticeship. Failing to write your story is the failure. The unwritten story is a tragedy. I don't presume to advise, but I will share advice I received as a new writer.

One of my first readers offered this advice when I'd written my first literary novel, after I'd sent the painstakingly polished manuscript out to publishers and agents. It had been a true labour of love, and because that novel was semi-autobiographical, it was hard not to take the rejections personally. The manuscripts trickled steadily back to me, the postman knocking on the door to pass me yet another fat brown envelope, which I added to the stack in the corner.

Many of the responses were what I called "rave" rejections, which funnily enough didn't make them easier to take. Editors and agents wrote phrases like: "it breaks my heart that I can't publish this book, but." But. It was too close to real life. It was too achingly sincere. There was no market for it.

And then came the advice. From one specific editor, at the end of her thoughtful letter. "But …I can tell you're a great writer. So keep writing. I'd love to see what you write next."

Keep writing. That was it, and that was all. It sounded so obvious. But bizarrely enough, it almost hadn't occurred to me before. As a debut writer, I had only focused on the book I had already written. But this editor had called me a writer. Of course, I WAS a writer.

And what writers do is write. Because surely I had another story to tell.

So I stopped worrying about the book I had written, and started thinking about the book that I wanted to write. Instead of looking back, I looked forward. I kept writing.

That next book was *Bitter Sweets*, the novel that got published as my debut. And my first editor, who gave me that advice, was the one who took it on. I've published six novels now. And as a published author, I've written six more manuscripts that never made it to publication. For many reasons, for being too experimental, or for having no commercial potential. But I'm not done yet and I'm never disheartened. I remember that advice, and pass it on.

You're a writer. So keep writing.

Because your stories are important. What we do is important, and we have to keep doing it. To create that storm. That flood. Break down the 'them and us', and invite the other to walk across the burning bridge.

I'm a small person. I have been dismissed, like everyone. I have suffered agonies of doubt, like everyone. But I have kept writing. Every day. I write because I must. I invite everyone to my world, and I have put people like me, my family and friends, at the heart of my fiction. I am a small person, but when I write I have a voice. It gets louder with every story I tell, and know it has been heard, and echoes all over the world.

If you'll permit me, I'd like to close with a personal experience, on the tragedy of the unwritten story. Before my father died, I met him in Paris. He'd lived an astonishing and wayward life, he had been a writer once, and always intended to write his autobiography. He told me he had finally completed it, that it was on a disc in his hotel. Two weeks later, he died in that hotel, and when my sister and I went to him, the disc in his case was blank. It took me ten years to write his story for him, the one he never told. It was this book, *The Flying Man*, and I'd like to share this small passage from the end.

(Reads from last pages of <u>Flying man</u>: "…A story for someone else to tell…wasn't there anything else you had to say to me? Wasn't there anything else that you had to say at all?… He pushes the door, which shines briefly about the edges, as though illuminated. He knows there is light on the other side.")

I urge you to find your light on the other side. Do not leave your story unwritten. Write with spirit. With passion. And keep writing, until you are heard.

And I cannot wait to hear the stories you create.

Roopa Farooki was born in Lahore, Pakistan and raised in London. She read Philosophy, Politics and Economics at New College, University of Oxford, and worked in advertising before turning to writing. She has published six novels with Headline and Macmillan, which have been listed for the Orange/Baileys Prize and translated into 13 languages. Her other award nominations include the Impac Dublin Literary Award, the DSC Prize for South Asian Literature and the Muslim Writers' Award. Her latest novel, *The Good Children*, was named "outstanding novel of the year" by the Daily Mail. She is a lecturer for the Masters in Creative Writing at Oxford University, and is currently studying medicine at St George's University of London. She lives with her husband and four young children.

SHAI HUSSAIN

This speech was made at the All Party Writers Group Summer Drinks Reception at the House of Lords on May 24th 2016.

Today, we're talking about diversity in the writing world, so I'm going to talk to you about the lack of opportunities for a heterosexual 34 year old, male Mancunian Muslim writer of a South Asian origin with a bad knee. #Diverse.

We all know that there's a problem with onscreen equality in terms of colour, age, gender, disability, sexuality and class. And the sad truth is that there always will be. As with anything in life, the result will never be perfect, but we can damn well try our best to achieve a balance.

In order to do that, we need to take an honest look at the level of diversity being commissioned, and more importantly NOT commissioned. There's an ongoing belief that stories about minorities just aren't commercially viable. However, the reason why they're often seen to be a risk isn't so much about the topic matter as it is regarding how much they trust a diverse writer to handle the topic.

Here are some of the best diverse British gems that have come out in the past few years: Luther, The A Word, Four Lions, Undercover, Indian Summers, Slumdog Millionaire. All amazing, all diverse underrepresented worlds… all written by white men with a proven track record. Should white men be exempt from writing amazing, diverse works? Obviously not. But are diverse writers getting their opportunity to prove their own track record?

Yes, a named writer will gain the project more credibility, an experienced writer will gain the project more quality, but the diverse voice that has lived the tale will give the story a strength just as important: authenticity. People say that diverse writers aren't commissioned because they're just not good enough. If you've never been commissioned, how are you ever going to get good enough?

The idea that diversity doesn't sell internationally? I have two words: Star Wars. A film with two leads who happen to respectively be black and female, and has made ooh £1.4billion. When we talk about diversity, it's easy for our eyes to glaze over. We expect kitchen sink dramas lamenting how poor and disadvantaged the life of minorities are. But that's only because those are the stories that get commissioned.

British Asian stories: terrorism and honour killings, with a sprinkling of a colourful wedding or Holi party. Black British drama is most likely set on a deprived council estate, guns and gangs. The disabled are rarely allowed to be 'normal', with their disability often being the main focus of the story. These shows only reinforce stereotypes. We need to aim for more adventurous storytelling and explore different genres outside of the kitchen sink. Characters don't need to be defined by their colour/religion/sexuality. Good writing is about universal truths.

So those were the problems. Now here's what you can do. Sorry, what WE can do. You don't have to be a woman to be a feminist. You don't need to be a minority to stand up for equal rights.

Number 1: Quotas. As I said earlier, TV diversity will never be a perfectly even spread. Taking this very speech as an example, I'm positive I've spoken more about BAME programming than other underrepresented communities. Quotas are good – they work as shown by the immense success of diversity in American TV, but we won't be able to fix the inequalities of everyone at once. The disabled currently need more exposure than any. And from my knowledge, the only - only - British TV series with a predominantly East Asian cast was a CBBC series called "Spirit Warriors". Released in 2010.

We can't allow political corrected-ness to go OTT where writing schemes guarantee one South Asian, one black writer, one East Asian, one bi, transgender, from Scunthorpe, female etc. regardless of talent. But we can address the imbalances one at a time.

Number 2: Ensure that the gatekeepers are always fully conscious of the levels of diversity at play – or even… this would be great…

Number 3: Recruit people from diverse backgrounds to be the gatekeepers.

Yes, diverse projects can be financially risky. But do you know what's more of a risk? Everyone turning to Netflix. More and more people are tuning out of terrestrial TV as they feel that it no longer speaks to them. I confess – I'm one of them. Give me Daredevil over Downton any day. For whole swathes of viewers to tune out could really dent the British economy. How's that for a financial risk?

Like its recent stand in politics*, Britain can be the diverse change it wants to see in the world. The talent is out there. It's just a matter of giving that talent the opportunity to shine. Especially if that writer happens to be a heterosexual 34 year old, male Mancunian Muslim of a South Asian origin with a bad left knee.

Sadiq Khan was just made mayor of London, which shows how recently this was written.

Shai Hussain has written for BBC Asian Network's daily radio soap *Silver Street*, followed by his play Reality Check and the co-written Resolutions. His afternoon play 'Til Jihad Do Us Part' was broadcast to critical acclaim on BBC Radio 4 in 2010 and he has adapted it for the big screen. He developed the screenplay *Company Sahib* with the support of Screen Yorkshire's Sparks Screenwriting Scheme, and is currently developing two sitcoms (*Small World* and *Boys to Men*) as well as a drama, *School of Sam*. His radio sitcom 'Generasians' has been optioned to NBC/Little Giant and he is now developing it for television. Shai has co-created a comedy drama series, *The Wedding Detectives* with fellow writer, Bill Armstrong.

THE HOPE OF A LOTUS BLOOM
C Iyengar
1st Prize 2018

It was the summer when power-cuts were punctuated by generator noises and the air-conditioners in barbershops hummed so loudly that children refused to believe that the electric razors weren't coming to get them. It was a time when Gita could actually feel her brain crumpling in the heat like a paper held to a candle flame. People held cold milk packets to their cheeks at dawn and by nine the stray dogs had found their respective shades and peed around them to cc mark their territory.

The corporation councillor had gone to Ooty for her summer holidays, mimicking the British officers who had escaped from the heat of the lands they owned and the ill will of the people they oppressed, a long time ago. So there was no one to complain to, about the power-cuts or the disappearing acts of the water tanker man, who sold the water to the rich patrons instead of bringing it to the residents.

Even if some officers did come to work in this sweltering heat and not tucked away in their bungalows with air-conditioning, they had far more important things to snore about. Many new officers started their careers in Gandhian fashion and soon realised espousing Gandhi's ideals was hard work and it wouldn't help them pay off debts – debts that sit on their backs like a camel's hump, debts that they had accumulated paying for the tuition teacher to pass their IAS exams, the debts their parents had accumulated getting them a posting in the corporation office and not the drainage department.

Gita switched off the fans just in case the power came back on while she was away and shut the door behind her. She crossed the street, her eyes focussed on the thin line of oil someone had spilled on the edges of the cement pavement that had survived the corruption of the contractors. She ignored the looks of the butcher's wife sweeping outside her house with a coconut stem broomstick. She ignored the pointed fingers of the old fortune-teller who spit deliberately as she walked past. A single dot of red splashed on top of her right foot. But Gita didn't stop.

The path curved towards the edge of town, where the auto-rickshaws sat waiting for a lone customer who might not know that the train station was just around the corner. The station itself was in the slumber of its rare busyness and irregular timetables. Gita had never had the chance to go anywhere on trains. No one to visit and nowhere to go. But she had stood there often and watched them pull away; taking passengers far away to places she wouldn't even know how to pronounce. What would it be like to get on a train and just go? She could be in Chennai or Hyderabad or even Mumbai before anyone noticed her missing.

She smiled at her own whimsy and kicked a stone on the pavement, watching it hurtle down the dusty surface. She turned left leaving that stone behind and walked to the ancient temple, crumbling by the weight of the banyan tree that grew through the cracks in its stones.

Gita circled the perimeter of the stone pillars and went to the back to the lake surrounded by stone steps. Birds from faraway countries used to come here for rest and food. Even as a child when they had visited her aunt, her father would bring her and point out the birds. He knew their names in Tamil and where they had come from. On the way back on the bus, he would draw the birds for her behind the bus-ticket.

But this summer, the monsoon had failed yet again and the summer was burning everything in its path unopposed. The birds had flown past without stopping. Dust swirled in the air and dewdrops had turned into mystical pearls that melted even before the moon set. The sun had scorched the greenness out of jasmine bushes and the redness out of the hibiscus. Its bright glare at first had shimmered in the lakes. Like a sly magician it had then soaked up all its watery goodness and revealed the brown nerve endings, jagged and broken.

And this is where Gita came to be alone. Like those migrating birds, she came to escape the winters of her aunt's dead eyes and drooping smile. She came to obviate the loneliness that had permeated the walls of her bedroom. She came here to avoid the pity of the old rickshaw man who sat at the end of the street, smiling at her kindly, every time she walked past.

She carefully stepped over the crumbling stone steps and found her spot close to where the water would have been. She could spot the bones of dead fishes, amongst the dried leaves and green moss that had been burnt into the floor of the lake. Like those fishes that had nowhere else to go, this life wasn't her choice. Gita had not only forced herself to endure it but she was also blamed for it.

*

When her father handed her over to his sister, as he breathed his last asthmatic breath, Gita hadn't pulled away. When her aunt had decided Gita would marry Anbu, her only son, Gita should have wondered why.

Anbu was a tractor salesman. He rode around the countryside on his Enfield Bullet showing the farmers the latest in tractors and tools. He carried laminated brochures, sales forms and a huge bag of goodies – from free pens to free torchlights.

He had taken her to the movies, bought her a new sari whenever he sold a new tractor and secretly brought her the special halwa from Pallipet and watched her eat, as he found her ticklish spots, where her sari revealed her mahogany-coloured skin. The lack of choice didn't seem to have bothered him either.

The newly-weds, a giggling pair could only hide the halwa for so long. Soon the mother-in-law smelled the ghee wafting through the room in the morning and demanded that all such special treats be sacrificed at the deity first and then to her before feeding the shameless wife.

Anbu surprisingly turned out to be one with the bite of a lion that matched the roar of his Enfield bullet. He found a house in the next town, and told his mother they were moving out. It wasn't Gita's idea – the mere sharing of the halwa wouldn't have severed the bonds of servitude to her mother-in-law. But Anbu didn't want to share the halwa or the giggles with someone waiting outside his door, eyes peering through the keyhole.

The scratch on the front door, the dying guava tree and the blame of the mother-son separation fell on the breasts of the unlucky daughter-in-law who had killed her own father and now looked set to murder her aunt too by taking her son away. Gita had remained silent.

*

In a new town and a new house, Gita busied herself with buying Anbu's favourite vegetables and fish in the street market. She saved up money here and there to buy the occasional chicken when she wanted him to be extra nice to her that night. She looked forward to the sound of the motorbike at the front door. She wore her new nylex saris he had brought back from his trips so he could slip them off her shoulders.

Then as Anbu's travels increased and his area office expanded, he worried about her loneliness and boredom.

'Don't worry, I'll dream about you,' she had said.

'That's not enough,' he said. 'You can't waste your degree and your typing diploma. Find a job.'

Gita could have found a teacher's job or a clerk's position at the municipal office if she had wanted. A corporation schoolteacher didn't need much more than her screeching voice and the times table. She could have taught a first standard class, and come back in the afternoon in time to watch the early evening soap operas on TV. But she was hoping that Anbu's passionate lovemaking will give her a baby soon and they could somehow placate her mother-in-law. What was the point of taking a job when she had to give it up in six months?

The house Anbu had found had remained empty for long. It was right next to a political party office. Especially the party in power. Then when Anbu found out they were looking for a typist, he had cajoled her to work there. I don't want you to sit at home all day, he had said. The alternative

27

was to go back to her mother-in-law's home to give each other company. Neither of them wanted that. Especially not Gita.

Her own body had betrayed her. Or perhaps the curse of the aunt was powerful to travel through the wind from one town to another. In spite of drawing the pitter-patter feet of Lord Krishna on the stone steps with rice-flour, in spite of the endless coconut offerings, there was no sign of a baby growing inside her. But Gita finally gave up on it and wrote her bio-data on a sheet of paper. Having run out of excuses and the monthly schedule of her womanhood unabated, she resigned herself to take the job next door.

A crow reminded her of the dusk settling in. She stared at the lake's parched skin like she would look into her grandmother's wrinkled face. But the lake had no new wisdom for her. The lines on the red earth didn't reveal any answers. But she did see a silent green stem of the lotus growing in the middle, in spite of the drought, in spite of the blazing sun overhead, where a little damp earth had escaped the fiery sun.

*

That summer had been scorching too. Just like this one. The whirring of the ceiling fan in the party office made everyone shout above it. The air-conditioning was turned on only when the big party leader from the capital turned up in a convoy of Gypsy vans and imported BMWs. For the rest of the mortals, the ceiling fan had to do the job.

On her first day though, Gita had worried about even entering the building. Party men of varying positions at the totem pole in white dhotis with party colours on the border and white shirts, stood aimlessly around, waiting for someone bigger than them to take notice. They often had the flag pinned to their chest with a safety pin and their shirt pockets sagged from two or three mobile phones. A dhoti with pockets had not been invented yet.

Betel nut stains surrounded the building like a fiery Lakshman Rekha. People waited in various poses outside the building – squatting, sitting, standing and even sleeping. All they wanted was their representative in the government would sign a letter, approve a form and listen to their woes. But hardly anyone listened. Gita found out later. Her job was to type up their requests and put it on the table of the ever-absent MLA. If he didn't use those requests to fold his toenails cut on top of the table, the infrequent visitor used it to fold the dry-roasted peanuts leftover from last night's shenanigans in the back room.

The first week she had cried with the old man who wanted compensation for the death of his son and with the old woman who wanted a death certificate to claim her insurance. That week she had bought the young woman a cup of tea as she listened to her stories of running from pillar to post, government office to minister's mistresses to get her case heard.

After a month, she had stopped listening. Now she was just a rock sculpted by the keys of the typewriter. She didn't absorb the words anymore. It had turned into a job that she could go in at ten and leave at four. Something to do when Anbu wasn't there.

*

Months later, it had turned into a habit. Gita hardly noticed the loud language of the politicians or the coarse cotton dhotis of those waiting in the queue. She came, she typed and she made tea for herself. She went home for lunch and came back after her allotted one hour. When left alone waiting for Anbu, she took out albums from his old metal trunk and looked at his baby photos, wondering whether her baby would look like him.

But there was no sign of a baby even though she read every book she could find in the second-hand bookshop or she followed every advice the spinach lady gave her – eat this, don't eat that, don't go on top, always stay under. The fortune teller with the parrot and a wooden stick with bronze tips had gestured without being asked, this side will give you a boy, that side will give you a girl. Anbu was amused when she told him to change positions. But he humoured her.

Even when she had rummaged around for the album, it had never occurred to her to look for secrets. She hadn't realised there was a secret in their marriage. The secret that her aunt had kept from her and ironically blamed Gita for, nowadays.

Anbu left home before eight and came back home before dinner. Sometimes he had to go further afield and couldn't return home the same night. He would arrange for someone from the party office to sleep outside her door. And when he did come back the next morning, he would nudge the guard away from the door, get into the house as quietly as he could and pretend they were in one of those matinee blue movies, only men and college students went to watch. They would stay inside until late afternoon, his one night of separation unquenched by a quickie.

It was one of those long trips that Thursday. Anbu would return only on Friday afternoon, and he promised to bring special halwa from another Pallipet on the way. He hung around the kitchen that morning, tickling her, teasing her and reluctant to go. Finally she had pushed him out of the house – 'Sell a few tractors and come back soon.'

She never found out if he had sold any tractors that day. His motorbike was found in a ditch near a farm somewhere miles away. The police had found him and due to her connections at the party office, they had brought everything back to her without pilfering through them. Even the mud-stained torchlights that said 'Vetri Tractors'.

It was in the death certificate that came in the post. The secret of her marriage, the thing that would have kept her awake at night, if she had known. The reason why her aunt married off her good-looking, moneymaking son to an orphan. The reason her aunt had accepted her with no dowry but a handful of bus tickets with drawings of birds behind them. Anbu had never told her about his epilepsy either.

Just like his own secret, Gita never got a chance to tell him what she had found out that Friday from the doctor at the Women's Clinic. A baby was going to enter their lives. But there was no life together anymore.

*

As the sparrows and crows returned to their nests by the lake, the sky slowly lost its summer glimmer. But the air was still humid. The baby kicked in her tummy, as if it could sense its mention in her memories.

Life was like the battle King Asoka had won. She had got what she wanted. But at what cost? There would be no more halwa from Pallipet or a new sari from Bodi. His fingers on her hips had been replaced with the flutter inside her belly and an ache in her heart.

The beat of the motorcycle used to race her heartbeat. It made her check her reflection in the mirror, adjust the jasmine flowers in her hair and wait for the gate to open, as it screeched on its un-oiled hinges. She spoke to the party leaders to get the motorbike back. One day she would hear its bullets thudding again.

Gita wanted to stay and work in the political office, unconsciously hoping Anbu would return one day to find her there. But she had more than Anbu's child with her. She had his duties too. Gita returned to her aunt with her things and the motorbike in a truck. She was welcomed by a fistful of sand in her face, her aunt screaming, 'You killed my son! You took him away from me. You will never live happily ever after.'

The last part was probably right. But not for the same reasons. Yet sometimes Gita felt grateful for ten months she had spent with Anbu. It was better to have stayed than taken the train.

There was no point arguing with the old woman who had lost her only son. She needed someone to blame. Gita let her. The blame was like the sweat that trickled down her face under the sun. It didn't hurt, but it coloured her skin and soiled her peace. She could wipe it all away but couldn't escape its humid embrace.

Her walk back home was slower and heavier. She wasn't looking forward to what lay ahead inevitably. She would cook dinner and her aunt would hurl it on the floor as she spit horrible curses that reverberated around the concrete walls. Gita never argued back. Nothing was going to bring Anbu back.

As she walked past the station, a train rushed past without stopping. Perhaps one day she would take one of those trains and find the world outside this town. Like the cranes that came from the far north. Like the rain that brought the whiff of the ocean in which it was born. Maybe one day, the healing will begin with the smile of the baby that had a bit of Anbu in it and a scar will appear where a wound festered now in her heart.

She and Anbu's motorbike would wait for the day when Anbu's child will claim it as their own. What if it were a girl instead of a boy, she asked herself. But she could hear Anbu laugh, his head thrown back and his eyes mischievous, 'Even girls ride motorcycles in the city. My daughter is going to drive an aeroplane.'

She sighed at her own reflection in a parked car. She too used to be a lake, shimmering and full of life. She touched her own little lotus gently, as she opened the door, bracing for a volley of insults that would erupt. Yet she smiled. All sweat dies in the cool breeze and all summers eventually melt in the monsoon. And her tiny shoot of lotus will soon bloom.

C Iyengar is an Indian-born British writer of many things. Her upbringing in India and its rich cannon of short stories and poetry in English, Tamil and Hindi has influenced her work. She also writes for children as Chitra Soundar and is published internationally. This is her first published short story in the UK.

FORMATIONS
Mona Dash
1st Prize 2017

Rukmini wills herself to stay lying on the sofa. *Om, Om Shanti*, she chants. The ghosts dance, screaming in a frenzy, wild shapes tearing at her eyelids, at her mind. Voices calling out as if to say, 'Come with us. We have come from far, we will take you away. Come....' As if a great breeze has whipped into the living room and is tugging at her hair, her clothes, as if the cushions will start to float soon. She keeps her eyes shut. Calmness, *Om, Om, Om*. Slowly they disappear, the anger in the room passes. Outside it is still dark.

It is November. Rukmini wakes at four in the morning in England, in her daughter's house, just like she did at home in India, except here the darkness lies deep and heavy. By the time the sun breaks through the greyness, and shines in its typical muted manner, Rukmini has done her pujas, showered, cooked the breakfast, and read a few pages of the Gita. Then Prasad wakes, and she makes some more tea; they like to drink endless cups of Earl Grey sitting on the flowered sofas in the conservatory, warmed by the electric heaters.

Today, she hesitantly tells Prasad about her experience.

'Once again? But how can you believe, even imagine, there are ghosts here?'

He points towards the houses on either side, the one on the left attached to theirs, the one on the right, a foot away, a dark brown fence between. Suburbia outside London, a place dotted with flowers and greenery. It's like holidaying in an Indian hill station.

'They are out there,' she points at the conifers at the bottom of the garden. The trees stand very tall making the house as private as a semi-detached can be. She has taken some time to understand the nuances; flats, terraced, town-houses, bungalows, semi-detached, detached houses.

'Don't mention this to Chaya. She won't be pleased,' he says.

'I have to. I want them out of here. They are creating havoc in our Chaya's life.'

Prasad is looking at Rukmini askance, his expression asks are you joking, but she looks serious. Since the last few days, she has been talking about the presence of evil spirits; ludicrous to think of ghosts in this calm oasis. He tries to stop his smile but it is too late.

'You don't believe me, do you? I will tell Chaya to get those trees cut.' She is convinced there is a vibration, a negative formation in the house. That is the reason Chaya's life isn't blossoming the way it should.

They hear footsteps upstairs. The acoustics in this house surprised them at first, every footstep, every whisper amplified. It is Chaya. They are confident they can differentiate between their daughter's footsteps and their son-in-law's.

Chaya comes in and slumps on the sofa. Her hair is a mess, curly locks wound over each other, just like it used to be when she was a teenager.

Rukmini starts without any preamble, 'Why don't you get those trees cut down?'

'What? Trees?' she stares outside as if she has just registered the trees. 'Why do you want them cut?'

Rukmini knows Chaya doesn't want to discuss this immediately after waking. She has been very busy at work for the last month, often leaving early and returning late. Yet she continues, 'It would look so nice and tidy.'

'Oh. But they give us some privacy,' Chaya says, her eyes narrowing, the way they do when she was feeling cross.

'But you would get more light in. You could grow vegetables, have a kitchen garden. It seems so eerie now.'

'Eerie?' Chaya gets up. 'I've left my phone upstairs, will be back.'

'What will you have for breakfast?' Rukmini calls out.

'Don't really mind. Doesn't matter.' They hear her run up the wooden stairs.

Prasad sighs, 'Did you have to tell her now?'

'It's a Saturday. They are both hardly around the rest of the week. When am I supposed to have a proper chat with her?'

*

It's almost ten am when Chaya and Satyan emerge. Satyan says in the over jovial way which Rukmini doesn't really appreciate, 'What are we having for breakfast? Puris?' He looks delighted at the stack of plump puris on the kitchen counter. She has made a light potato curry; the way he likes it. Her son-in-law declares himself a foodie, and loves her cooking, unlike Chaya; she will just have cereal – not even cornflakes with warm milk and sugar like she did as a child – but unsweetened muesli, sometimes a croissant and coffee. For lunch, even on weekends, she insists on a salad, cuts an avocado in half, chucks its round ball of a seed into the bin. The cold food her daughter has surely can't be helping her.

Later, much after breakfast, when Rukmini is surveying the fridge to decide the menu for lunch – and thinks of making some fish cutlets, Chaya comes around and says, 'It's happened again.'

'Don't worry, it will happen soon.' Rukmini wants to reach out and stroke her daughter's face, so delicate, fine-featured, to hug her slim body, which she takes to the gym every other day, but her daughter stands a foot away, her shoulders slumped.

Chaya laughs cynically. Rukmini knows that laughter. The one Chaya launches into whenever she feels lost and it is so often that her youngest child feels like this. Quick to despair, quick to lose hope, as if the grief was only hers to bear, as if no one else could understand.

'How soon is soon for you? It has been a year and half already.'

'What does Satyan say?'

'He is fed up, Ma. He says if it has to happen it will, but he can't take this stress any more. He thinks I am being obsessive, and all this is adversely affecting his work.'

'Why don't you go to another doctor?'

'He just said we should give it up.'

'Another doctor could help, maybe an IVF...'

'But my gynaecologist is the best, don't you get it?' she stomps away again.

Prasad is blissfully watching something on the telly and smiling to himself. Rukmini comes up to him.

'She is upset. No luck this month also and Satyan isn't being supportive.'

'But the doctor says the tests are normal for both...and what is Satyan's issue now?'

'I told her to change the doctor.'

'You did not! You know she is upset. First the trees, now the doctor. How could you?!'

'Well, if you know what should be said, why aren't you there to say it? I was only trying to help. Eighteen months and nothing. Surely the doctors should do something? Why, remember my friend Minati? Her daughter in America did an IVF, within months had twin girls. She was thirty-eight! Chaya is still a bit younger.'

'It will happen. Surely my daughter will not be so disappointed in life. God can't be so cruel.'

'I have already promised I will light a thousand diyas in the Jagannath temple, if she conceives soon.'

'How soon?'

'I don't know. You can't demand that way.'

She looks out of the kitchen window. In the daylight, now that the sun is higher in the sky, everything looks innocuous. Some autumn flowers, she doesn't know the names of, have bloomed, very colourful but with no fragrance. But she cannot forget the despair of the night, it had felt so solid. Something in the house which prevents anything good from happening. Something that isn't right.

She thinks for a while and decides she will do a puja to drive away the ghosts. She will cook Chaya meals with warming Ayurvedic ingredients, then her daughter will surely conceive. She needs to eat some food cooked with love, food from her childhood. She writes her list for the time they will go to the Indian area to stock on groceries.

*

On Monday, Chaya walks out of the house briskly and walks ten minutes to the station. They moved here two years ago from the heart of London, like people do, when they want

38

to start families. The landscaped gardens, the parks, the many young parents pushing prams; the ambience can do nothing when nature isn't willing. After a while, sex becomes just that, mere contortions in bed with no purpose, every month her period comes right on time like a trusted friend. Five days after the onset, the ovulation thermometer indicates she is at her most fertile; she has to force Satyan at times.

'I have a headache tonight,' he said once. It struck her as ironic, a man using the age-old excuse of a woman. He went to bed, two Nurofens later. But in the morning, she reminded him, 'Still at the most fertile.' He turned over and dutifully pushed the liquid out of him.

'Something is wrong with the angle perhaps,' she had said, propping her bottom on pillows. She feels sticky drops on her thighs. 'I am not sure if anything is staying in.' 'That's the way it is I think,' he said, getting up swiftly for a shower. No more of the soft kissing after they were done, no more lying across his chest, talking pasts and futures. The act had to be dutifully done twice a day to maximise chances. Except that nothing worked.

Now she gets on her train, doing her make-up with swift strokes. She gets out at London bridge, walks up Southwark street, and through Borough market, past skinned rabbits and plump cupcakes, past purple kale and gutted seabass, up to the flat with its blue door. She knocks and he is there in a second.

'Right on time as usual,' Ronan says.

The minute he shuts the door, she is in his arms.

'Hmm, you smell of toast,' she says. 'Warm toast.'

'And you smell delicious as always.'

'New perfume though!'

'Perfume takes the smell of skin; did you know?'

On the couch, warm orange, they divest each other of everything they are wearing, a stone jumper, dark red trousers, blue jeans, grey t-shirt; all in a heap. She feels fierce, she feels needy, and Ronan knows her well, knows how to calm her body, her frantic mind and set her back into the day.

They leave together, but in separate directions and he hands her a paper bag, her favourite almond croissant, he gets them from the little café Mabel's, down the road.

'I am so hungry, thank you.'

*

The fridge is filled with tiny boxes with lids. Rukmini looks into one and finds some dried pasta shells stuck to each other, as if put into boiling water, but removed hastily.

'Why do you have all these little boxes of food?' she asks Chaya. 'Can I throw this?' She rattles the box.

'I thought I might use it when I make penne again.'

'But will you? Why not just throw it as you will possibly forget it's there, isn't it?'

'Don't like wasting food,' she says, walking away. It makes Rukmini smile. Why does Chaya worry about a minor wastage when they indulge extravagantly otherwise? The number of shoes Chaya owns is mind-boggling. The other day, they were in Oxford Street, and she walked into a large store, and within minutes was out, with a Topshop bag. A pair of shoes, some skinny jeans, a sort of lace top, she said.

Rukmini wishes her daughter could shop for baby clothes instead.

*

Now, for Chaya, Rukmini makes rich curries, she stirs cream into chicken, she steams fish, marinates in mustard sauce then bakes in tender leaves, fries eggs in butter – 'Will she eat any of that?' Prasad comments watching her labour in the kitchen.

'She has to. This will make her fertile, warm her insides. None of that cold angrez stuff she keeps having. Would she agree to pack some for lunch, do you think?'

Prasad laughs so loudly that she turns back to the simmering pot. In a restaurant, at lunch one day, Chaya had ordered some Moules mariniere mussels she explained to them as if it was part of their daily diet. She scooped the tiny bit of flesh expertly, one mussel after the other, and Rukmini commented, 'How can a daughter of mine eat a bowl of seashells and like it?' they had all laughed. The next morning at breakfast, Chaya's eyes were clouded again, her words angry red. Rukmini told Prasad, 'Another month of failed trying. Poor things.'

For the spirits, she makes the special black laddoo. She rolls flour, sugar, purple food colouring, and folds the secret powder mixture of cinnamon, nutmeg, almonds, into small perfect balls. She will offer them every day in the puja, and later give it to Chaya and Satyan to eat.

*

Chaya has a message from Ronan, can she come for a while in the evening? She leaves work a bit early, and meets him at the Rake, one of his favourite pubs. He wants to cook tonight and stops for some fresh egg pasta on the way to the flat. He likes cooking for her; he arranges salami, prosciutto, cheeses on a platter, cooks anchovies in olive oil, and grates courgettes into ribbons for her prawn linguine.

41

He serves it on the round marble table by the bay window, and she lights candles. Once he bought oysters from the fishmonger, and showed her to how to slurp all the saltiness, aren't oysters the best aphrodisiac? she joked. He works as a creative director in a production house and she feels his creativity touches everything he does.

'I can't stay for dinner tonight though. My parents will be waiting,' she says. She has been staying overnight when Satyan is away. Some of her spare clothes nestle in a drawer in the bedroom.

'Can I meet them?' He is smiling, his hands clasping hers.

'Wouldn't that be good?' she sighs, wondering what they would say if she introduced him. Her mother, scandalised, her father, more patient. But their eyes would fill with shame. How could you, our son-in law is a gem, they would say.

'But why can't it be Chaya? Why can't I meet them? Why can't you tell them?'

'Don't start that again.'

'But we have to talk! Where is this heading?'

'And I thought that was meant to be the woman's dialogue.'

'It's not funny Chaya. You need to decide.' He has stopped. He is looking at her, into her. His hands are on her waist.

'It wasn't meant to be serious when we started. You had a girlfriend, remember. Sarah, I think.'

'It was never serious with Sarah, I used to meet her on and off, and you know that. I was only trying to get over Dawn. After five years with her…'

'So you used Sarah to get over Dawn and now it's me…who are you getting over?'

'Don't you even think of going that way. You know I am not using you. You know…'

And she does. She knows how he feels for her. Some months earlier, they met at a mutual friend's birthday in a crowded wine bar. Later they would try to deduce how they had ended up in the same cab going back to the friend's flat. Satyan had been away on one of his long work trips and she had stayed like many of them, drinking into the next morning. Ronan and she exchanged numbers, though they hadn't met, until months later at the same friend's again. 'Nothing serious, just once,' she had said, when that night, very drunk, they had kissed out on the terrace. But they hadn't been able to stop. For a month now, Ronan has been saying, 'Leave him. We have to give ourselves time. We have to see where we can go.'

'It's hard,' she says now. She has said this before.

'But why? You don't love him, do you?'

'It's not about love.'

'What is it about then?'

'I want to have a baby.'

'Well, someday. But now…we need to have some time together.'

'I am trying to have a baby, I mean.'

He is silent for a minute, then she sees comprehension in his eyes. Light-brown eyes darkening like the skies did when clouds rose in them, like the time they did when he was in bed, his arms around her, his lips on her.

'A baby…with him?' He stares.

'Well, yes. I am not getting any younger. It needs to happen soon…you know, I have been trying so long, it's so frustrating.'

His hands drop off her, and he walks away.

'I don't have the time to wait darling,' she moves closer to him. He is thirty-one, and it is odd for her to be with someone younger than her. He said age made no difference, she had to think beyond.

She follows him, and reaches up to kiss him. 'Make love to me,' she whispers. In the flat, they cling together legs, arms, faces, mouths, tongues, thighs, as if one, on the couch, the pile rug, the bed. But afterwards, he raises himself on his elbows and looks at her, 'Do you tell him that as well, to make love to you? How can you?'

'Don't start. This is about us.'

'You need to decide Chaya! Now or never! You can't go on like this. It's not fair to anyone – him, me or even you.'

She scoops her dress from the floor, pulls it over her quickly, and leaves.

She is hungry, she walks past the Roast where they have dinner at times. The first time, when she ordered a steak, he said, 'I didn't know Indians eat meat. The Indian guys at work, and even at uni, are vegetarian.'

'Let's say I am not your typical Indian!'

'But you grew up there?'

'Of course, but we come in different shapes and sizes! Jokes aside, the 'vegetarian' or 'non-vegetarian' depends on which region you are from. However, I am not meant to eat beef. My mother would be horrified.' She had laughed as the blood broke when she cut her rare steak.

'There's so much to know about you. Will I ever?'

That is the first time she had sensed he may want more. The first time she had sensed she may want him to want more.

*

44

She hurries home now, looking at her phone every couple of minutes. Nothing from Ronan.

The smell of cooking is strong as she walks into the house. They are just getting ready to eat.

'You must be hungry.'

'Yes, I am – starving.'

Her mother looks surprised, but so happy, that Chaya feels guilty she hasn't been enthusiastic about the extraordinary spread she has been making for the last few days. Now she ladles king prawns cooked in a rich masala of onions and ginger, aubergines fried in circles, white rice, yellow dal, minced lamb with peas, on a plate.

'Too much, Ma,' Chaya protests.

'Eat while you can, you won't get all this when they go back in a few days! My mother-in-law is such a good cook,' Satyan laughs.

'What have you eaten for lunch today?' her mother asks.

'Crayfish and avocado salad. Pret.'

'All this cold food isn't good for you. Nice warm Indian food is what you need.'

'Eat up, eat up,' her father says.

After dinner, he says, 'Have a laddoo, also.'

'Ma has made laddoos?'

'Yes, for a puja,' Satyan says. 'I had one as well.'

'Why are they…well so black?' A few black balls are placed in her best china bowl.

'Just a special type. Do you like it?'

'Yes Ma, it's all great. I loved the prawns. Just like when we were younger.'

'It was always your favourite, beti. We all need our childhood food, it completes us. It's our manna.'

45

She thinks of Ronan alone in his flat having dinner. She texts him goodnight from the bedroom.

*

She wakes up to the smell of something frying, she hears the oil sputter, Satyan's voice, 'Upma today! Lucky us.'

'A warm breakfast is what you both need. I am making some nice coffee as well, Indian style. None of this cappuccino stuff for Chaya,' she hears her mother say.

She has never liked upma, though her mother makes it well. Black mustard seeds, thin sliced chillies and fragrant coriander leaves in white grains of semolina. She spoons some into her mouth, wanting to knock on the blue door instead, share a flaky croissant from Mable's and remove the crumb gently from the corner of Ronan's lips. With him she feels she has enough. The baby which doesn't come, pulling at her, haunting her all the time here in the house, disappears. Once she has baby hands in hers, maybe she will be able to forget Ronan. But what if she never has a baby? Then, will her life with Satyan ever be enough? She checks her phone, still nothing. Isn't he missing her? She heads to work.

*

'See, she is eating so much better now. She has to come back to her roots, eat the food she is meant to, and soon she will conceive. Wait and see. They are both looking happier, don't you think?' Rukmini tells Prasad. 'Now let me go outside, do the puja and offer laddoos to the spirits.'

'You think everything is about food and prayers,' sighs Prasad.

46

'But it is!' she starts to gather ingredients for the puja. On a bronze tray, she arranges a pot of incense sticks, a diya, the bowl of black balls, the little puja bell, and some of the orange flowers from the borders outside.

*

Halfway to the station, Chaya realises she has forgotten her phone. She can't spend all day without it. She rushes back, she's left it on the dining table perhaps. The house feels strangely quiet. Where is everyone? Then she notices the conservatory door is open, her father is outside watching her mother who is right at the back of the garden. She is sitting cross-legged on the grass, smoke curls from some incense sticks, a diya burns with a bright flame. Her mother tries to shield it from the light breeze that flaps at her saree. Her face is rapt, her red bindi so prominent in the greyness. Everything is still; a single autumn leaf flutters down.

Suddenly her father turns and sees her, and says, 'Sssh...sssh,' he gestures and comes inside.

'What on earth does Ma think she is doing?'

'Just a puja, don't worry, she means no harm, it's all for you.'

'But why is she sitting there... on the grass?' she can't help but laugh. 'This is really crazy!' A gentle tinkling sounds as her mother shakes the puja bell.

'You know her...she always means well..,' she sees his eyes grow with affection, his smile grow until he also starts laughing.

'I know,' she stands close to him watching her mother.

He says, 'Your phone...it's been ringing, quite a few times.'

'Is it?' she picks up the phone, looks at it and smiles.

47

Mona Dash writes fiction and poetry and her work has been anthologised widely and published in international journals. She has a Masters in Creative Writing (with distinction) from the London Metropolitan University. Her work includes *Untamed Heart*, her first novel and two collections of poetry. Mona was awarded a 'Poet of excellence' award in the House of Lords in 2016. Mona has also participated in readings in venues such as Lauderdale House, Nehru Centre, the House of Lords, The Library, Yurt Café all in London and in literary festivals such as Leicester Writes, Durham, Rochdale and Wolverhampton Literature festival. Her short stories have been shortlisted and longlisted in various competitions such as The Asian Writer, Fish Short story, Strand International, Words and Women, UK, to name some. Mona leads a double life; she is a Telecoms Engineer and a MBA and works full-time in a global technology organisation. Originally from India, she lives in London.

THE SWIM
Jamilah Ahmed
1st Prize 2016

The perimeter walls of the American Compound were at odds with the rest of the city of Dubai. The stone was dark. It had been selected to stand out against the soft desert background. The houses here had sloping roofs and small chimney outlets, which had no function beyond the decorative. Sand gathered in the crevices, and solidified into salted crusts. At their coffee-mornings, American housewives would swap tips on how best to combat this problem, and discuss how their maid or gardener could keep the exterior tidy. They hadn't considered removing these unnecessary appendages.

Ameera liked having a friend who lived on the American compound. On days spent at Christine's house, she lived an expat life, and stepped outside her own family ways. Leah pulled up outside the house, and Ameera ran in, saying hello to Christine's mother as she made her way to Christine's room. The bedroom had posters of boy-bands on the walls with 'I love A-Ha' written in black marker, and kisses in smudged red lipstick. As Def Leppard or Bon Jovi shouted from the speakers, Christine would tell Ameera of the latest development in her love life. There were several boys on the compound with whom she was allowed to go on dates. These dates were sanctioned by Christine's parents as long as they remained within the walls of the compound. Recently however, Christine had grown fascinated by the US marines who were invited into the compound on 'home-visits'. Both girls knew that this transgression could have serious consequences. Ameera wondered if everyone was pushing at the boundaries of their worlds, asking to be let into another place, if only for a while.

Christine began to load blue eye shadow onto her lids, puffs of it floated down to the desk. She wore a bright yellow pencil skirt and a loose black t-shirt that slipped off one shoulder, revealing a blue bra-strap. Ameera looked down at her own skirt, soft pink with a paisley print that flowed down to her toes, in their flat black shoes. Her outfit had pleased her this morning, now she felt out-of-place, like an extra from *Little House on the Prairie*. Christine's hair was hard with hairspray, and Ameera realised there must already be a plan for the day. Christine shut the door and jumped cross-legged onto the bed beside Ameera, 'Do you want to meet Serge today? Come for a bit, and then let us have some time to be alone?'

Ameera stared at the blue eyes. She had no interest in meeting this latest crush of Christine's, but wanted even less to be on her own, while Christine spent time alone with a marine officer. Christine carried on, 'There's a BBQ we can go to, and you might meet someone there too. Then Serge has said he wants us to be alone! Can you believe that? He wants me!'

Ameera felt repulsed, she didn't think she could bear to meet this American man who said such things to her friend. Sometimes Ameera thought nothing happened, sometimes she believed Christine's tales of body-to-body exploration. She looked blankly at Christine, 'I don't want to meet anyone, I will come for the BBQ so I know where you are. But this isn't a good idea. It's going too far.'

Christine hugged her knees to her chest, her make-up smudged as her eyes crinkled with excitement, 'I can't believe he's chosen me! It's the best summer of my life!'

Ameera picked at the cookies left for them by Christine's mother. This was not the best summer of her life. She did not want a world in which everyone grabbed at what was outside their reach. Maybe her father was right, maybe it was better when things stayed the same, in their 'proper places'. But such phrases belonged to another time, they held no power now. Christine offered her the eye shadow brush, 'Shall we get ready?'

Ameera took the powder and dabbed some around her lashes. The blue looked ridiculous around her dark brown eyes, and she rubbed it off quickly. She found a black eye-pencil in Christine's make-up bag and drew hard lines around her eyes that smeared into the corners. She looked at herself through half-closed lids, sideways on. She looked different from when she had arrived, older. She would not have been allowed to leave her own house with such make-up. Ameera took a bottle of bright red nail-varnish from another small zipped bag. The gloss hardened and dried, transforming her hands into someone else's. She would have to take it off before she went home.

When Christine was ready they went to tell her mother they were going out.

'How's your mum Ameera? She didn't stop for a chat when she dropped you off this morning, which was a shame. Is she well?' Sheila often asked Ameera's mother in for a coffee, or spent half an hour outside in the sun, leaning into the car as they talked. Christine prodded Ameera impatiently, she replied quickly 'Yes, thanks, she's fine.'

'And you? How are you? I thought you did very well at the Inauguration Ceremony you know. That's a lot to take on, a recital and playing in the orchestra I thought you managed very well.'

Ameera didn't know what to say to this, clearly she had not managed well but gave the answer she felt Sheila wanted, 'It was OK, I'll practise more another time.'

'Don't you worry about it petal, I'm sure your mum and dad are proud of you.'

Ameera pushed her face into a smile and followed Christine out into the sun.

As they walked, Christine recounted her conversation with Serge the previous evening, adding details that left Ameera increasingly less enthusiastic about the afternoon ahead. They neared the clubhouse and were spotted by the hostess, Christine's neighbour Martha. A short wide woman with a helmet of dyed black hair, who bowled over and engulfed them in a hug, 'Girls, I am pleased you're here! We're about to light the fire and you can help Billy and Chuck!' She laughed loudly as if a funny joke had been shared, and ushered them towards her son and his friend. Behind them, Serge leaned against the wall, his tall frame casting shadows on the pool surface. As they talked to the boys, Serge walked over and asked Billy if he needed help with the BBQ and so the game began. Christine and Serge were the leaders in this dance, and Ameera and the two teenage boys mere buffers between the couple and the adults. It was sad, thought Ameera, that Martha could not read the dynamics of this group, was not alert to the role of her own son as pawn in an elaborate game.

When they all sat down to lunch, the dynamic abated slightly. Christine was irritable now that she was no longer the focus of Serge's attention. She hardly spoke to Ameera and they ate at each other's sides in silence as the adults talked around them. Serge talked of his weekend leave spent at Martha's house, how the time spent in a family home gave him renewed vigour once he was back on the base ship. Ameera wondered how many others were on the ship, how many naval officers came ashore and meddled in lives before they disappeared, literally, into the horizon. She was worried about the afternoon he and Christine had planned. He had nothing to lose. He did not belong here, the rules did not hold his world together. She watched Christine, her laughs louder at his jokes than anyone else's, her wonder writ large on her face.

After lunch they headed into the clubhouse café for ice-creams, and Serge suggested a walk down to the beach. Ameera knew this was her cue, even before Christine's blue beacons signalled this was her moment. The boys turned towards the pier in search of new playmates and Ameera said bye to Christine and Serge, who walked away, towards the far end of the beach.

Ameera sat at the ice-cream bar. She had hoped that a day spent with Christine would rid her of her thoughts, not leave her alone with them. She tried to think how to occupy the next two hours, until Christine returned, and they could go home again. The shop had filled up now, groups of friends milling around looking for ice-cream and entertainment. Ameera watched them, and listened to their jokes and banter. Her ice-cream finished, she bent down to reach for her bag, but her elbow brushed into the man next to her, a smudge of his bright pink ice-cream glowed on her arm.

'I'm sorry, here have my napkin.' He wasn't American, he smiled but knew to look away, not to embarrass her with too long a gaze. Ameera took the napkin and mumbled her thanks as she walked quickly out of the shop. She started walking away from the crowds and was about to throw the napkin into the bin when she noticed a scrawl on the edge of it. A shot of recognition trilled through her body. She had always discarded such notes quickly in the past, as if holding them for too long would taint her. Today, alone, she read it carefully: 'Deen 0770 347457 call me'. She scrunched the napkin quickly into her hand and kept walking, past the bin. She looked down into her hand, and read it again, as if the ink might have faded in the few minutes. She didn't look back, but pushed the napkin in to her bag and zipped it shut. She walked on until she reached the end of the compound, the rusted metal fence stretching out to sea.

She was away from everyone now, only a lone swimmer at the periphery of her vision to distract her. She didn't know if his splashes were bravado or the inelegance of a poor swimmer. I could do better than that, thought Ameera. She looked back along the empty stretch of beach, the pier was far away and she could not tell if the small dots that moved back and forth were men or women. They would not be able to tell who she was. She stepped out of her long skirt, and unbuttoned her shirt. Ameera stood on the beach, in her black vest and long black leggings that she wore beneath for modesty. She wondered if from a distance she could pass for a scuba-diver. She smiled, imagining a new trend in swimwear for local women. Ameera felt her face twist in amusement, the movement seemed from a long time ago.

She walked forward into the sea until it reached her armpits, and she could hardly see the bright red nail varnish on her toes. She ducked under the water, and let herself sink almost to the bottom, around her tiny fish burrowed into the sand, alarmed at this invader from above. She pushed upwards and took in a big gulp of air. As she wiped the salt-water out of her eyes, and pushed her hair back, Serge's face came into focus, it refused to leave her thoughts. She ducked back under the water and continued to swim, came up for air and then disappeared again as she followed the line of the fence beneath the sea. Every time the face reappeared she ducked under the water again, until it came to her no longer. She swam on, leaving the end of the barrier behind as it dipped beneath the surface. She could swim out of the compound if she wanted.

The water was cooler now that she was further from the shore. Far out, on the right, the naval ship hovered on the horizon, a small dash against the clear sky. Her limbs began to ache as she swam into the waves. To her left Ameera could make out the pier. She had no idea what time it was. She swivelled round in the water. She floated onto her back and let the sun dazzle her eyes as she squinted upwards. Her feet and hands paddled gently as she absorbed the sounds and sensations of being surrounded by water. A sense of peace crept into her, it filled her entirety and pushed out, at last, the turmoil of the past few weeks. She stared up at the sky, Christine, Serge, her squabbling sisters, and even her father all seemed tiny and distant.

Out here, she was more alone than she had ever experienced. She flipped over onto her belly, legs straight and her heels dipped up and down with the tide. No-one could see her. If she put her mouth and nose into the water, she could eliminate the shore from her vision. Wave after wave tipped over her and towards the beach. Ameera let her body sink into the water, and felt the sea lap over her face, like a blind drawn down over her face, it closed off the means to talk, to listen, to discover. She wondered how long it would take before they would notice she was gone, how long it would take before her limbs could float no more.

Jamilah Ahmed was born in Dubai and is half Arab, half Irish. She has lived in London since graduating from University. She has a PhD from Goldsmiths, where her work examined the female embodied self. Jamilah works in publishing, previously as a Commissioning Editor in the social sciences and more recently as a freelance editor and agent. Her writing career began with an OU online course. Following a *GoldDust* mentorship, her work has been longlisted by *Mslexia* & *WriteIdea*, and shortlisted for the Si Leeds Literary Prize 2016.

SEASCAPES
CG Menon
1ˢᵗ Prize 2014

It isn't until she gets to the bus stop that Deepa knows her feet are wrong. They're aching a little under the hem of her sari, but that's not it. Perhaps they're just tired; she's already trotted along miles of vinyl corridors behind the hospital tea trolley and trudged through the evening's drizzling rain. She sits down, shakes her legs, and reads the graffiti daubed on the concrete wall. *Alex Loves Sara.* She likes that, hopes he does, but perhaps Sara wrote it herself. It's been that sort of day.

She frowns at her feet again. They're throbbing and damp and somehow she thinks they shouldn't be here at all. They should be fins instead; green and scaled and shimmering, with a shiver of muscle running down to the tip. It's an old trick from her childhood, when she used to sit on the damp concrete outside the Marina swimming pool in Madras and pretend to be makara. A sea monster. She used to go further, pretend she had the swirling peacock feathers, the doomed and tragic eyes. Not any more though; not here.

But for a second she feels just like a makara again, and she examines those sturdy ankles that swelled when Rahul was born and haven't really gone down since. She hadn't thought that sea monsters had feet, but perhaps it doesn't matter in the end, and so she picks up her shopping and climbs onto the waiting bus. In the distance the Tyne swirls in an eddy of turbid brown.

She remembers another river, diamond-bright as it bubbled over her toes. A stream, really, with a bed of stones polished to smooth curves. She remembers the hillside near Middlesbrough, sloping and littered with greyish flints, and the distant factory chimneys that puffed out clouds of pure white smoke. Sheep-white and grass-green and sky-blue, she remembers, and the sun beating down forever on the clover that stained her hands.

She shifts her grip on the string handles. She's got cod for Bill's dinner, and she thinks she could stretch it for two days with some dal. Bill's not too fond of dal though – calls it fancy foreign muck when he's down at the pub, but he's gentle too; he tries to make sure she doesn't hear.

They'd had dal that day too, dolloped into lukewarm plastic containers and squashed with the chapattis into her mother's leather bag. That bag had come across with them all from Madras the winter before – Amma and Appa, little Anil, Deepa, Karthika-chechi with her woollen cardigans. All of them left a bit battered; all of them frozen and brown in a grey-white city.

And on their very first family outing – and this was the point in the story where Amma's eyes widened and her voice dropped with a delicious swoop – Deepa had got lost, somewhere on that steep green hillside. It's part of the family folklore, like when Blackie ran away or when Anil was summonsed for cycling without a light.

'When we called to fetch her back, she was gone!'

The suspense didn't last long. She'd turned up half an hour later playing with flints and in a tantrum about being found at all. But Deepa knows there's another part to the story, broken off like a jagged tooth in the back of her mouth. There's a part of the story where she wades upstream to a rocky crevice covered in fairy-green moss. Hidden deep within the spongy softness she uncovers a cleft where the water springs fresh and bubbling, finds a cavern just behind it that teems with nymphs and sirens with fish's tails. She dives in through the stony lips; she's tossed by waves and ground against rocks until she emerges polished as flint and changed into something else entirely.

Bill's waiting at home when she arrives, sitting in his old brown armchair by the television. She keeps meaning to have the place redecorated, but you can't get that sort of flock paper nowadays, and plain paint reminds her of the slums.

'It's fish tonight, dear.'

She struggles out of her coat, the solid shape of her hips and shoulders stretched into the cloth, and runs cold water over the greasy breakfast dishes. Bill *will* leave his plate on the table, egg drying out and toast crumbs down the front of his shirt. He's kind, though; she gives him his due even inside her head, as the gas fire starts to warm the chilly kitchen and the fish splutters in the frying pan.

She shuffles back through to the living room, where Bill's chisel and hook knife lie on the table next to a half-carved toy horse. Something for Katie, Rahul's first, and such a pretty, fair girl, but she's getting far too old for wooden toys. She hopes Bill won't mind. Since he retired from the carpentering he likes to keep his hand in with carving, but it's all Lego and Sindy dolls now, and to tell the truth he never really was that good. He was a practical carpenter, turning out solid objects that lasted. She's glad he's stopped, she thinks, stretching her toes inside her worn carpet slippers and wishing for fins. There are already too many things in this country that last.

'I can't even swim,' she says abruptly.

'Eh? What's that, pet?' Bill leans forward and switches off the set, looking at her with puzzlement. She can smell the fish smoking away in the kitchen – it'll be burnt, but he'll chew through it manfully and never notice.

'I want to learn how to swim.'

He eyes her warily, and she can see he's wondering if this is the change. She's too old for that though; went through it ten years ago and had the house turned upside down with her sweats like the monsoon.

'They have those aquarobics classes,' he ventures. 'Down at the baths.' His eyes are bleary but he's trying to please her, and so she sniffles a few times and hurries back to the kitchen to sit with her dupatta pulled over her head and listen to the dinner burning.

It's raining the next day, a cold drizzle, and her fingers are numb as she moves about the kitchen straightening things up. It's her day off, and someone else will have to dole out the polystyrene cups of scalding tea and feel the edge of Annie Higgs' tongue. Annie's got cancer, lies drenched with pain on a crumpled pillow and calls her a Paki when it gets too bad, though Deepa's never been near Pakistan in her life. She says she's just waiting to die, but Deepa knows differently. She'll hang on a good few more years, long past the time when Deepa herself will slough her skin and swim off instead with a monster's tail polished bright as an iron lung.

Bill's in front of the television again, puffing out yellow fug from his pipe. She's been asking him to stop for years, but he likes the feel of the stem in his mouth, and anyway, he spends more time fiddling with it than smoking. She used to mind the circle of dusty grey around his armchair where the ash grinds into the carpet, but by now she's used to it. Occasionally she imagines coming back home one day by herself, turning the stiff key in the door, wearing her white sari for the first time since her wedding – Bill's mam insisted, said it was the proper colour for brides, and Deepa had practically grown up here anyway, it wasn't as though she was really *foreign* – and seeing that island of ash.

'I found you those swimming classes,' Bill announces. He's been up since five; he doesn't sleep much anyway and he's pleased to have a reason to be up out of the roil and muddle of the tangled bed sheets. She frowns. She knows what she said last night, and it's true – she thought she was a makara, and it's not as though you can be changing much at her time of life, so she supposes that she still is – but she no longer thinks that swimming will get her anywhere.

'Three o'clock.' He hands her a brochure that must have been sitting in the back of a drawer for months, along with a takeaway menu and a notice about council meetings. 'Senior Citizens Aquarobics', it reads. It's bright and glossy, with a picture of some smiling, shining nymphs: senior citizens in bright pink bathing caps. They're poised on the side of an ominously blue pool. *Don't jump*, she thinks – thinks of lemmings and suicide pacts and village girls flinging themselves from mango trees with rope around their necks. 'Classes at 3pm'.

She examines the picture dubiously. Perhaps somewhere in that chemical blue there's a rent, a gap where she can slip through to the palm trees and storm-filled skies of Madras, but she doesn't think so. All those ladies look too solid for that. They look like they're built to last.

Nevertheless, she agrees to go and have a look. Do some shopping, have some tea in town before she comes back to make the jam roly-poly for tonight. Bill would like her out of the house for a while, she knows. His sports programme is on soon and she's been edgy, snapping at him and burning the fish last night, although he'd never dream of saying so.

She takes a small rucksack with her, takes one of Karthika-chechi's old cardigans and a book for the trip. The pamphlet Bill gave her has the route to the baths, but she doesn't need it. She's not going to town, to aquarobics and shopping and tea. She's going back to find those stones that cut like glass and that spring that bubbled out of the fresh-tasting earth. She's going to scatter everything to glory with a single flick of her peacock tail, breakfast plates and bathing caps and bunions and all. She's going back to Middlesbrough.

She thanks the bus driver as she clambers down at the station to catch the express. He's a young lad, with a shock of hair like Anil before he went into the navy and cut it short and got himself killed in that accident out in Australia.

'Middlesbrough' says the board on the next bay, and so she climbs onto the express bus and tugs her blouse down against the cold. She has no picnic this time, no dal in plastic containers, no cold chapattis to stick to her fingers, nothing but a cardigan and a cheap rucksack, and it worries her. This is a journey. She should have taken provisions.

A few more people shuffle on to the bus. It's half past two on a bright Tuesday afternoon, and that's a *definite* time, a time for appointments and grocery shopping and bank managers. It's a time to be jotted in a diary with a ballpoint pen, but these people don't seem to have any plans at all. She rummages in her rucksack as the bus rolls out and finds a barley sugar. She unwraps it, and then, sucking, drops the paper deliberately on the floor. It's her own form of graffiti – *Deepa was here* – and she wishes she'd thought of it earlier. She dozes, and wakes to find that they're trundling along a valley floor just outside Middlesbrough. It's dark now, and hills rise on either side with their tops still lit by the flattened rays of sunset. The sloping ground is littered with flints and criss-crossed by wavering drystone walls, and there's a cairn on the highest hillside. It's a tottering pile of rocks that catches the sun with a reddish glow and sends a shadow stretching like a finger towards the road. She rings the bell hurriedly and hopes the bus stop is nearby.

She'd thought she would recognise somewhere, remember something, but the bus has come to a juddering halt, and there's nothing left to do but climb down and stand under the fluorescent tube of the bus shelter. She's stiff now – too many hours on that seat – and her jauntiness has ebbed away to leave a strange, spreading misery. She's small again, she thinks; she's frozen and brown; she's fancy foreign muck.

The hillside rises gently, close-cropped grass scattered with rabbit droppings just becoming visible in the pallid moonlight. There's a remembered taste in that rising wind: Royapuram harbour after a storm. It's an old taste, a salt-and-decay taste of storms and weed and ocean slime, and murky waters covering things best left forgotten. Cars roar past on the road below. She's high enough that their lights only catch the edge of her coat, and she thinks with pleasure that she must resemble something quite natural – a rock, a tree – and not Deepa at all.

She reaches the cairn, still warm from the sun. Round the leeward side it's windless and calm, and she lowers herself down against the stones. The air here is quiet, and the grass has grown rank in long, weed-like strands that break under her fingers. The rocks against her back are colder than she'd thought, and feel less secure. Like the drystone walls – like a lot of things built to last – there's nothing holding them together.

Just over that rise, she thinks, there could be a little rocky gully with a bubbling stream and a crushed smell of clover and that miasma that rises from the grass at night. She could walk to the very edge of the cairn's long shadow and tug off her shoes, barefoot in the warm dust in the way she remembers. She could wade along the river, past the sharp-edged stones, and the silvery tadpoles and the splash and gurgle of great eels, past the bow waves of gigantic fish, past the worms hundreds of metres long and the flattened serpents that churn and coil in the current. She could be swept off her feet by the tidal surge, swept over a bottomless chasm of water the exact colour of her monster's tail.

She pulls her sari straight and settles back further in the grass. She has some things to leave, and here's as good a place as any. She doesn't expect to miss them, but just for a second she feels strange. Like a lemming, she remembers thinking a long time ago. Like a suicide pact. Like a village girl in a mango tree.

And so she leaves a sea monster here, under the stones where she can hide until her skin gleams new as copper. She leaves a bride, dressed in red and gold and all the colours of the sun. She leaves Annie, who's never seen a hospital trolley in her life; and Alex, who loves Sara and always will;

and Anil, who came back from the navy and wrote them every single day.

It must be an hour later by the time Deepa stands up. The wind has risen, and she begins to feel her way through the flints to the bus shelter below. Bill will be wanting his dinner, she thinks, and starts to count ingredients in her head. One egg, two eggs. Suet for the jam roly-poly.

CG Menon has won the Bare Fiction Prize, the Leicester Writes Prize, The Short Story Award, the Asian Writer Prize, The TBL Short Story Award and the Winchester Writers Festival award. She's been shortlisted for the Fish short story prize, the Short Fiction Journal awards, as well as the Willesden Herald, Rubery and WriteIdea prizes and the Fiction Desk Newcomer award. Her work has been published in a number of anthologies and broadcast on radio. She is currently studying for a creative writing MA at City University and working on her first novel.

THE GARDENER
Jocelyn Watson
1st Prize 2013

Never in a sari. On Sundays she'd always change first. Back from mass, she'd unwind the six yards of silk or chiffon, replacing it with her baggy black cotton tracksuit and her brown pumps. Even in those unflattering clothes, her black eyes and quiet grace shone through. Her features were as prepossessing and loving as her physical accomplishments in her garden. She'd look round with a satisfied smile at the fruits of her labour before coming indoors, where she'd infuse the house with aromas of jeera, haldi, cinnamon and cloves. Then she'd call out to us. 'Anthony.' She get no response.

'Angelo.' Sometimes he would oblige if he wasn't working on his Meccano set.

'Maya.' She was Ma's best bet if she wasn't in the shower or on the phone.

When no help was forthcoming she'd call out again.

'You children. Can't you hear me calling?'

If we were together upstairs, or with Pa in the TV room, we'd mouth her words, and laugh. Then I'd be told to go.

All Ma wanted was for one of us to go out into the garden to pick – kari pattha – curry leaves which she'd throw into a saucepan of simmering curry. Actually, thinking about it now, Ma wanted more. She wanted us to look at her garden and her kari pattha tree. After she had thrown the kari pattha leaves into the pot she'd head upstairs, and change into a home sari: simple, comfortable and usually unembroidered. After lunch we'd watch some old black and white Hollywood movie in the TV room. Ma loved Rita Hayworth. Pa'd sit on his Parker Knoll, Ma in her armchair and the four of us squashed up together on the sofa bed. As the credits opened with the huge cymbal sounding, or the cock crowing, Pa would break into a gentle snore while Ma would remind us, for the umpteenth time, that Rita Hayworth was Indian.

When they returned to England, finding a house with a garden had been a priority for Ma. She wanted to make up for all the years she hadn't had a garden in Hong Kong. Despite her affection for all that blossomed in her garden, Ma longed for a small kari pattha tree. She wanted something of India in her garden. Over the years she would take fresh kari pattha leaves, root them as stem cuttings, willing them to grow but, more often than not, they would droop and die.

Once when I was about eight, I came into the kitchen and saw Ma looking at her kari pattha with such sadness in her eyes. I remember rushing up and hugging her and telling her, 'Don't cry, Ma. They're only leaves.'

'Oh sweetie, but they remind me of home.'

'But Ma this is your home.'

'Yes, darling.' She patted me on the cheek. 'But I have two homes. You have three.'

'This is my home.' I straightened my back and stared at Ma.

'Of course. But your Papa is English, I'm Indian and you were born in Hong Kong. So you have three places in the world you can call home.'

I remember walking out of the kitchen wondering whether I liked the idea of three homes or not.

Pa would make the four of us smile, when he complimented Ma about her garden. He knew how to take care of the gardener but never did any work himself. Whenever he saw the blossoms on the trees, the flowers in full bloom, he'd tell Ma her sunflowers were as rich as Van Gogh's or her roses as red as her bindi and Ma would smile. When he told her that her jasmine or her oriental lilies, smelt as sweet as she did after a bath, she'd give him one tight slap. We were clear it was Ma's garden, though we all enjoyed it in different ways. Anthony and Angelo played football when they were younger and sometimes if Anthony got into a huff he'd storm out, walk round, and return in a calmer frame of mind. When we were kids Ma would hide chocolate eggs for us to find at Easter. In the spring and summer we'd put out folding tables and chairs and friends would come over for lunch. She even filled the 'hungry gap' with leeks and curly kale until her spring vegetables were ready to harvest.

Ma'd try to cajole the four of us into helping her in the garden, and then when her grandchildren were old enough, she would try, unsuccessfully, to rope them in. Occasionally, one of us would cut the lawn or weed a bit, though it never lasted for long. If Maya or I had something we wanted to talk to her about: sleepovers, trips, parties, we'd wait till she was in the garden, and then we'd follow her round, chatting away before launching into whatever it was that we wanted. We were such fools; as though Ma didn't know. She knew, but she just liked us following her round the garden. Unless it was something crazy like: Maya, at fifteen, wanting to go to the Kumbh Mela; with a few cautionary words, she'd agree.

Eventually Ma gave up on us all, and through St Xavier's, the local Catholic Church, she found Malcolm. Malcolm was a quiet, broad shouldered man who, though originally from Dublin, now lived in Larkden. Malcolm became Ma's gardening soulmate. They were always engrossed in discussions about: the soil, the compost, the frost, the bugs, the weeds, her new plants, *Gardeners' Question Time*, or something they'd read about. When we were young, it was the sixties and though people ate curries they didn't really know what went into them, and rarely cooked curries for themselves, so there was nowhere, in the little Hertfordshire village of Larkden, to buy Indian herbs and spices. Ma was determined to grow her own kari pattha but Malcolm, though he knew a lot about growing plants and herbs, had never heard of kari pattha.

*

It was one summer Sunday when I could have been no more than nine, so Maya was eleven, Angelo thirteen and Anthony fifteen. We came home from mass. Though not as stunning as Ma, we all had to wear our best for church: Maya and I wore dresses with coloured tights and the boys suits with ties. Pa stopped the car outside the house. Normally one of us had to pull up the garage door but that morning Pa told us not to. We got out of the car, grabbing the keys from Ma, ready to change into our shorts. As soon as we got through the door Pa reined us in as though we were cattle on the loose.

'No dawdling. Change. Put on something comfortable but decent and be quick about it.'

We all stood there staring at him.

'Why what's happening?' Ma asked

'No questions. Hurry up now.'

We all stood there like statues. It was so unlike Pa; on a Sunday he read the *Observer* from cover to cover before lunch. We each had our routine; Pa's orders just didn't make sense.

He pointed us upstairs. Anthony and Angelo put on jeans and a T-shirt, so Maya and I did the same. Ma put on a green going-into-town sari, not too fancy but nice enough, and Pa bundled us back into his sea blue zephyr without giving anything away. We whispered in the back, and as though to placate us, Pa put on Radio One, moving his shoulders about to the rhythm that made us laugh. We kept asking but he wouldn't tell. When he'd had enough of Radio 1, he got us playing games. I remember us shouting and giggling in the backseat as we vied to see who'd win. After two hours Pa finally stopped and parked the car. We looked out but none of us was any the wiser. Then Ma threw her arms around Pa and we all looked at her in surprise cos Ma doesn't do that kind of thing. Anthony and Angelo were more controlled and patted Pa on the back. Maya and I just smiled at him as we didn't really know what to expect as we'd never been to Kew Gardens before. We understood it was for Ma's benefit, though by the end of the day we'd all enjoyed ourselves. Our first stop was the café where Pa said we could have whatever we wanted so we had scones and ice cream, chocolate and pop much to Ma's disapproval. Pa coaxed her into having a scone with her tea and we laughed as she struggled to open her mouth wide enough to bite into it. As we walked past the Pagoda, Ma saw an Asian gardener and she ran towards him. We were all rather shocked but followed behind and stood watching her. She told him her worries and he shared all he knew. It made Ma's day; she was thrilled.

Not far from Larkden are a number of garden centres. The next day Ma went by herself and bought what she needed, cut the stem cleanly at the node, and pushed the cutting a few centimetres into a mixture of potting compost and aquarium gravel with three curry leaves above the surface, as he had recommended. She planted it next to her bay leaf tree having decided they would be good company for each other. Months later she called Nana in Poona to tell her that her kari pattha was growing well. We were chuffed. From then on, if it was cold she'd cover it with a blanket, and talk to it regularly, about India, I imagine. The result was she always had fresh kari pattha. When she retired, the love and energy she had devoted to teaching her primary school classes, was now focussed on her garden. When Pa passed away it was gardening, the piano and her grandchildren that gave her life meaning.

*

While we were working through Ma's things: the boxes in the loft of ornaments, mementos, letters from India, from Hong Kong, from her travels around the world, her clothes in the cupboards, her saris in the Chinese camphor wood chests, I realised what would be lovely, would be something from her garden. We had to sell Ma's house so I knew it couldn't be anything that damaged its appearance.

I would have treasured the willow tree that drooped lovingly at the front of the house. Like most Asian families we had relatives scattered across the globe: India, Pakistan, America, Canada, Australia and Africa and they'd always want to be photographed by the willow tree. There didn't seem to be a part of the world where Ma didn't have relatives or friends. Once she'd settled whoever in, she'd sit with them in the living room, looking out onto the garden. If the weather was nippy, she would simply point things out otherwise she escorted them round, as though giving them a tour of a country estate, not a small back garden.

*

The removal men came and loaded up boxes, a sofa, a bureau and a leather portfolio of Ma's paintings. She'd have laughed; her paintings of her flowers and trees that I have since framed, now line my staircase. I point them out to all my visitors.

'These are paintings my Mother did.'

When I tell friends, 'she didn't start painting until she was eighty, and what she loved painting most of all were the flowers and trees in her garden,' they look again with a tenderness that her work deserves.

*

Her eighty-fifth birthday, the last birthday she was able to celebrate, was here in my Tottenham flat. Her birthday's in July and we were fortunate that year; it was a bright, sunny day. Her good friend, Ena drove her over. While we waited for my sister to pick up our Auntie Marie from Eltham, we sat on my little verandah looking across at the park. She advised me about my hostas, pink geraniums, and the elegant Japanese Acer she'd brought me three years previously for my birthday. When everyone had arrived, we sat out on the balcony. Ma pointed out all the new plants in the neighbours' gardens and in the park ahead and finally when we'd finished off the birthday champagne, we came in for dinner. The grandchildren helped their Grandmother blow out her candles on the cake I had ordered from Belle Epoque, that she loved for the colourful garden design, I'd specially requested, and the others loved for the delicious melee of rich dark chocolate, cointreau and berries.

Ma loved growth. She didn't aim for a particular design just a feast of colour, as lavish as the precious stones of her noratin jewellery set, that I remember Pa buying for her in Bombay when I was six. Ma's garden had bright yellow marigold, pale Lords and Ladies, red poppies and blue lilies, tissue paper white peony blooms. The flowering of her fuchsia rhododendron bush always brought an outpouring of delight. When we came to visit we would sit in the living room, admiring the vibrancy and radiance of Ma's garden and watch the robins, thrushes, sparrows or the occasional red cap woodpecker helping themselves to the nuts Ma provided for them in their very own bird house.

*

Before the removal men arrived, I looked in the back and front searching for what I might dig up and replant on my balcony. Something I could cherish. The others were busy going through drawers and cabinets, emptying and filling boxes. If I dug up the roses in the front, or the boastful sunflowers, the entrance would look naked. The clusters of delicate red begonias, purple hyacinth, orange cannas and pink chrysanthemum were so perfectly positioned. There was nothing I felt I could lift without doing irreparable damage to Ma's front garden so I turned to the back, and just kept looking, till Kartini called, 'Auntie Josephine your removal men have arrived.'

I took them into the kitchen for a cup of tea before showing them round the house.

'What a beautiful garden your Mother had.'

'Yes,' I replied almost tearful.

I identified the stuff I wanted them to take and dashed round to the back garden again. I could've happily taken the white bird house, held up by a solid wooden pole. It could've leant against the railing of my balcony but I didn't have the heart; Ma had already donated it to the birds.

Before long one of the removal men came out. He was a big, weathered man, with heavy, blunt hands and tattoos of something Gothic and dark running up both arms. He came and stood beside me.

'We've put everything in. Is there anything else you want us to take?'

I stared at him, distraught. I couldn't leave without something from Ma's garden.

'My ma passed away not long ago. I know it happens to us all, but it was the hardest journey I've ever been on, and I've been on a fair few.'

I remained there unable to move.

'Are you sure there's nothing else?'

'I don't know.'

'You want something from this garden, don't you?'

'Yes. But I don't have space for that slender silver birch or that dome shaped apple tree.'

His eyes travelled round the garden. 'Where's it for?'

'My balcony. That's all I have.'

'Well what's that next to the bay tree? There,' he said, pointing at the kari pattha tree.

Knowing how Ma had struggled all those years to grow the kari pattha, it seemed sacrilegious to take away that little part of India that she had planted in English soil.

I shook my head.

'What about that bay tree next to it? That'd fit in neatly.'

'Yes,' I said with relief.

'Did your Mother keep her shovels over there?' he asked pointing to Ma's white shed.

I nodded.

'Well I'll grab a spade, dig it up then cover over the hole. I'll wrap up the roots. We can pick up a pot and some compost on the way back to yours and I'll replant it on your balcony.'

Tears streamed down my cheeks.

'Is that not what you want?' His eyes opened wide as he stared down at me.

'No, yes. Yes, very much. Thank you.'

'Well, why don't you go in and check if you've forgotten anything and I'll sort this out. My mate's happy having another cuppa with your sister and brothers and the kids.'

Ma's bay tree is now replanted in a big wooden tub on my balcony and how it's grown; the leaves are a deep, dark, emerald green.

*

A year ago Ma's house was sold and we returned to Larkden to sign various papers at the solicitor's office. It was a relief to have finally settled Ma's estate and once we finished, we had lunch in the Peking Chef, Ma's favourite restaurant. Maya then suggested that we drive past for a last look.

'What a good idea,' Anthony said.

We jumped into the car and were off down the road and up the hill. We all smiled at each other as we turned the corner of Bellingham Lane into Turnstile Way.

'No.'

Angelo was silent.

'How could they?'

I just stared. They had ransacked Ma's front garden. The willow tree, the gladioli, the roses, the clusters of delicate red begonias, the purple hyacinth, the cannas and the chrysanthemum, even the proud yellow sunflowers; all gone, destroyed, paved over; a grey mass of concrete and two parked cars.

'I'm sorry I suggested coming.'

Anthony put his hand on Maya's shoulder. 'It's not your fault.'

When I returned home, I went to the balcony. Under the dusty orange sky I stared across at the plants and Ma's bay tree. I reminded myself that reality isn't static; nothing's fixed or permanent, but I was lucky; Ma had gifted me a garden full of memories.

The Asian Women's Writers Collective was **Jocelyn Watson**'s first writing home. In 2001, the Women's Press published her first short story, *Menaka*. In 2011 she won a Jane Austen Short Story Award for *Poske* published by in *Wooing Mr Wickham*. Jocelyn is one of the Alumni of the Cultural Leadership Programme and was funded to attend the Jaipur Literature Festival in 2011. In 2012 she was one of the winners of the SAMPAD *'Inspired by Tagore'* competition for *Loud Music* and the Asian Writer Short Story Prize for *Sweet and Sour Masala*. She is active in feminist, BME and socialist politics.

EASY TO FORGET, EASY TO REMEMBER
Deepa Anappara
1st Prize 2012

When the woman with a stern voice announces the imminent arrival of the Swarna Jayanti, Rashid rolls up the sleeves of his only red shirt, revealing a series of matching red cuts running the length of his hands. For a second it worries him that he does not remember how he acquired the marks. Then he laughs at himself. Over the past few days, he has plunged his hands into dust-bins, stacks of rubbish, and a drain under the pavement where he sleeps. Anything could have caused these cuts. He should be grateful his fingers are still intact.

He spits on his cupped right palm and, with the bubbly saliva, polishes the already-gleaming 'licensed railway porter' badge tied around his left bicep. The badge belongs to Kareem Chacha, who bought it in the black market for sixty-thousand rupees five years ago. Once in a while, when Chacha's back snaps like a dry twig after he has balanced one too many suitcases on his head, he loans Rashid the badge until his pain ebbs. They share the money Rashid makes, which is embarrassingly not much, because though he is younger than Chacha, he tires easily.

Through the white fog that cloaks Ahmedabad, Rashid catches a glint of the train in the distance, and prepares to dive into the darkness of its AC First Class compartment just as the wheels clickety-clack into the station. The glue he sniffs daily makes him less alert than he would have liked to be for this particular task. Still, he races the Swarna Jayanti as it pulls in, dangles by a railing next to a thick iron door

78

for a few seconds, his feet dragging along the platform, and then somersaults into the compartment, bumping against impatient passengers waiting to get down.

'Sorry, sorry,' he says as he burrows inside the chilly compartment. He slumps down into a side berth instead of grabbing the bags of passengers before they can protest.

By the time his heart has stopped punching his chest, the train has stopped, and other porters have negotiated their rates with those who have heavy bags or are too frail to carry their own.

'Oh my god, is that you Rashid?'

Zainab is the only woman who calls him by his name, but surely she cannot be here? He rubs his eyes and peers at the shadowy figure. It is Kalpana Ben, who looks older and different. Her face was once smooth, but now it has multiple folds and wrinkles. Her hair, which was black and thick, is grey. When he stands up, he spots an unsettling bald patch on her scalp that she has failed to conceal with hair meticulously combed over it.

She runs her hand over the inch-long, whitish scar on his left eyebrow, the remnant of a scrap in his childhood, and says, 'It's providence. Our meeting like this. I was hoping to find you.'

Rashid helps her with her bags.

'Where do you live now?' she asks. 'I spoke to your uncle a couple of times and he had no idea. He said you ran away from the Dharwad school?'

Rashid smiles and heads out of the compartment. If he answers her questions, she will turn up at his side every day, with the same orange candy she used to shove into his mouth when he was as a child.

*

Unfortunately for Rashid, Kalpana Ben is so resourceful that she locates the exact spot on the pavement where he sleeps, and pays him frequent visits at odd hours of the morning. Over the years, he has learnt to sleep through the rumble of buses, the growls of bikes, and the vibrations that shake the ground each time a truck passes, but Kalpana Ben does not hesitate to wake him up by sprinkling water on his face. It terrifies him at first. Though he is no longer a child, he feels as if he is back in his old school in Dharwad, waking up to another bully teasing him even before the day has begun. Soon he will have to jostle against fellow students to use the bathroom, head to the dining room to eat clumpy upma, then onto the classroom where he will be caned for failing to learn Kannada, a language as foreign to him as English. He had disliked that school so much that he had run away, a fact that disappoints Kalpana Ben no end.

The first few times, she talks to him kindly and asks after his health, but possibly from the stink that hovers over him, she gathers what his weakness is.

'You have to stop sniffing glue,' she takes to shouting like a politician pleading for votes. 'Don't you see it's killing you?'

Rashid does not expect her to understand. Certain things he has to do to live on the street. He cannot sift through garbage and find something to eat if he is sober. He cannot drop his pants when someone bigger than him orders him to do so. He cannot fall asleep in the cold (and Allah, it is so cold these days). Only Zainab, who unzips his pants at night and makes him happy, understands. Like him, she appreciates the soothing qualities of glue, the way it blurs the shape of one's past and makes the present bearable.

Kalpana Ben has no idea what glue can do. When Rashid inhales quality stuff like Dendrite, he turns into a butterfly. No, a bird. He rises above leaves spinning in the air and collides against soft white clouds. Zainab waves at him from the pavement. She is so tiny, he can fit her in his beak. The cars on the road appear like ants that he can crush at will.

*

Some mornings, Rashid wakes up wishing he could pick wallets like his friends Javed and Mustafa. They go around the city, travelling ticketless on buses, cadging rides from tempo drivers, or hanging from the back of lorries, their shirts billowing in the wind. They have an elaborate routine: Javed sheds tears over an imaginary wound, dances like a film star, or offers to polish shoes, distracting gullible men, while Mustafa cleans out their pockets. Rashid tried it a few times, but he was rubbish at it. He was too nervous, too eager to run away. He stopped going with them though he sometimes misses the excitement. Like when they told him about stealing a freakishly-tall White man's wallet, with green money in it, at the Sabarmati Ashram of all places (Mahatma Gandhi ki jai ho!). They were rich for weeks.

Because he is a coward, Rashid has to work so he can buy himself a bottle of whitener. He will try his luck with Kareem Chacha today. He wraps up all his belongings in his blanket, so he can leave it for safekeeping with Althaf, who works as a cobbler on the other side of the pavement.

'Rashid,' Kalpana Ben calls out to him. 'Where are you going?' She tugs at a line of wool that is unravelling in the red sweater she wears over her salwar-kameez.

'I have to work.'

'Do you know what next Wednesday is?'

If she lived on the street, she would know that days and dates do not matter to him. His ears pick up rumours about police raids and road repairs, and he arranges his life so that he is not around when the bulldozers arrive. Some people go to the mosque on Fridays but though Rashid calls on Allah a lot, he remembers the afternoon prayers only when he hears the maulvi's voice over the loudspeaker.

'On Wednesday, it will be ten years since your parents were killed,' Kalpana Ben says as Rashid scans the road, hoping the traffic will pause for a while so he can cross. 'It's the tenth anniversary of the riots.'

Rashid does not know why she calls it an anniversary. It is not an occasion for a celebration.

'Can't you be clean at least for one day? To honour their memory?' she asks.

As if to appease him, she tries to push some candy down the front pocket of his shirt though it is torn halfway. He brushes off her hand.

Kalpana Ben seems to like reminding him that his parents were killed in the riots of 2002. A thousand others, or two-thousand others (as if anyone bothered to keep count), were killed in that dhamaal. Rashid refuses to dwell on those days. Instead he thinks about flying. One hit and he will be high for a good half an hour.

'Look, Ben,' he says. 'I need to make at least twenty-seven rupees today.'

Immediately the creases on her face become deeper. He is such an idiot. Thirty, should have said thirty. Twenty-seven is such a precise number that she knows it can only be for one thing.

'Let me see,' she says. 'Twenty-seven rupees will get you, what? Fifteen millilitres of White Ink?'

He smiles because she has done her research. He reckons he will make a run for the other side, but just as he puts his foot down on the tarmac, a big car whizzes past, letting out a loud, unremitting honk. Its tyres barely miss his leg. Kalpana Ben grips his elbow.

'Rashid Beta,' she says, her voice low and soft, as if speaking to an injured animal. 'Let me help you.'

'You will give me thirty, no, forty rupees?' Now that he thinks of it, he realises he does not have the strength to cart suitcases around. He feels the twinge of a headache, probably brought on by this woman.

'Last time I got you money, it was a cheque for one lakh.' Her voice has developed an accusatory tone that annoys Rashid. 'What happened to it, Rashid? Do you know?'

His uncle had pocketed the government compensation, then sent him off to the boarding school in Dharwad. When Rashid came back to Ahmedabad, he had claimed to be ashamed of him and had thrown him out. Living with his uncle would have meant going back to school, probably one run by strict, cassock-wearing Christian priests, so Rashid had not been unduly bothered. Allah knows he hates school.

'We had such high hopes for you,' Kalpana Ben says. 'Don't you remember how you shared a stage with the President of India? He thought you would become a doctor, or an engineer. Wait, there's something I want you to see.' She rummages in her bulky bag for a couple of minutes and triumphantly pulls out a laminated newspaper clipping. 'See, this here' – she jabs her index finger at the clipping, which baulks and folds under the pressure – 'is you.'

Rashid examines the clipping carefully. The article is in English, so he cannot read it. But the photo is big and he can see himself clearly. He looks smart in trousers and a full-sleeved, striped shirt – he remembers the clothes had been a gift from Kalpana Ben's NGO – and he is sitting on the President's lap. The President's long silver hair is parted in the middle and falls in ringlets, framing his face. He has bushy eyebrows and a slight paunch, and looks like a magician. Now Rashid recalls his naïve belief that the President would make mobs disappear.

He had accompanied the President to the jhopadbhatti where he lived. Pointed out his burnt home to the perfume-and-paper smelling official contingent. Walked around glass shards, scattered pots and pans, and a table that had its legs up in the air as if pleading for mercy. The President had squeezed Rashid's shoulders and told him to study well.

He returns the clipping to Kalpana Ben.

'They're asking about you,' she says.

'The President?'

'He's no longer our President,' she snaps. 'Rashid, just listen, okay? A TV channel wants to interview people who were very young at that time. To find out how they're doing now.'

'Tell them I'm doing just fine,' Rashid says. Then he dashes past honking, screeching and swerving cars, and laughs as drivers fling insults at him like water balloons.

*

Allah is his witness, Rashid has never thought of going back, though the jhopadbhatti is less than an hour away from his pavement. Until now, he has not wondered what happened to his neighbours or the boys with whom he played cricket, hide-and-seek and land-water. But here he is, showing Zainab the watermark on the boundary wall of the government school where he had studied until the third standard. He tells her about the monsoon months when brown water from clogged drains sneaked into his house and eventually rose so high that he feared it would drown him.

'But you were able to miss school,' she says, as if it was a fair trade-off.

The jhopadbhatti lies behind the school. The burnt houses he last saw here are gone. Instead, there are rows of tin sheds that sometimes share walls.

They walk under metal staircases leading to wobbly, first-floor extensions leaning towards the earth as if in desperate need of a good night's sleep. On the lane, a carpet of red chillies has been laid out for drying. Zainab mischievously steps on a few and grins at Rashid as her slippers disembowel the chillies, releasing yellow seeds. They can hear the sound of televisions, a mother crying in an afternoon serial, a father lecturing his son in a Hindi film. A friendly dog follows them.

Standing at her doorstep, a woman empties a bucket of soapy water that she must have used for washing vessels onto their feet, and turns back without an apology or a smile. Rashid's feet are already cold and now he shivers. Though it is afternoon, the sun is mild, shielded by the slanting roofs of the tin sheds and the tarpaulin sheets tied above it. Clotheslines flap above their heads.

'Let's go,' Zainab says. '*Those* people live here.'

Rashid peers through a half-open door and spots posters of many-armed Hindu gods and goddesses stuck on the walls. A little boy lies on the floor watching television.

'They forced us to leave, then moved into our homes,' Zainab says. 'Your home reeks of their incense now.'

But all Rashid can smell is Dendrite, so sweet and intense that it makes his heart race and his head feel light. Holding Zainab's hand, he walks back to his old school, which is lying locked. Must be a holiday today or a Sunday. They scale the boundary wall in a section where it has crumbled. Then they climb the stairs to the terrace, and look down on the jhopadbhatti they just visited. They see: girls sitting on beams of sunshine, swatting flies, their bangles sliding up and down their wrists; women chopping onions, their legs spread out on the charpais edging their homes, wiping away tears with their saris; punctured cycle tyres and bricks placed on roofs to keep the tarp from moving in the wind; and stray dogs and goats slurping water from muddy puddles.

'This is how it looked years ago,' Rashid says.

'Are you mad or what?' Zainab asks. 'We're nothing like them.'

For years, Rashid has depended on glue to blur the world, but images — some still fuzzy, some sharp — hurtle towards him like fallen stars. Once he starts remembering the harshness with which his father boxed his ears, the tenderness with which his mother cooked him lunch, where will it stop?

'Here, take it,' Zainab says, holding something in her outstretched hand.

Rashid steps forward and squints at an orange-red spinning top.

'It was lying outside somebody's house. I picked it up.'

When he does not respond, Zainab diligently wraps a string around the bottom-half of the spin-top. Balancing it in her hands carefully, she throws it to the floor, where it starts spinning around an invisible line.

Rashid thinks he may have seen the spin-top outside the house of the boy watching television.

'You stole it?' he asks.

'They're living in our houses. What do you call that?'

The spin-top begins to wobble.

'I saw them die,' he says.

'Who?'

'The mob set fire to my father's beard first. I didn't scream, because I was scared they would see me. I was hiding inside a sewer pipe.'

Zainab picks up the spin-top, which has toppled over. She flings it from the terrace, onto the tarp-covered roofs of the tin sheds below them. Then she pulls a blue plastic pocket out of her blouse and holds it up. Rashid grabs it from her, presses it against his nostrils, and inhales. He waits to be lifted above the earth, though he has to acknowledge that sometimes, the higher he is, the clearer everything becomes.

Deepa Anappara is currently doing a PhD in Creative-Critical Writing at the University of East Anglia, Norwich. She has a Masters in Creative Writing from UEA and previously worked as a journalist and editor in India. Her novel-in-progress, *Djinn Patrol on the Purple Line,* won the Bridport/Peggy Chapman-Andrews Award for First Novel in 2017, the Lucy Cavendish Fiction Prize in 2018, and the Deborah Rogers Foundation Writers Award in 2018. Her short fiction has won: the Dastaan Award, the Asian Writer Short Story Prize, the second prize in the Bristol Short Story awards and the third prize in the Asham awards.

MOHSIN HAMID

This interview first appeared in The Asian Writer on August 2007

Your last two novels took seven years to write. What keeps you motivated to keep writing?

For me it's a couple of different things. One is the hope that I will finish this thing and have some love at the end of it and the other thing is this desperate need – I wouldn't know what to do if I wasn't writing this stuff. It keeps me sane. There has never been a choice but that I have to keep writing. So when seven years ago I was in the novel writing process, certainly there are times where you're in despair and you think 'Oh my God, is this going to get anywhere?' and you go through all of that, but I think the fact that I had to do it in the end and I kept remembering what my goal for the project was.

I understand you've had other jobs while writing, is that true?

Thank goodness 'cause otherwise if you spend seven years on a book and you don't do anything else you'd starve to death – so I've worked throughout my writing career. My first novel I began writing in 1993 I was a law student for a while, and then I worked in consultancy firm in New York for a while till 2000. Since 2000-2007 while I was writing my second book I worked as a brand consultant in London, then as a management consultant in New York and as a freelance journalist in Pakistan and a full time writer.

Sounds like you're a very busy person. What's your writing ritual?

It's more now that I find my best writing is first thing in the morning before I check my emails, before I open the newspaper before I do anything to distract myself. It's first thing in the morning that I'm my most productive. So my writing ritual really is to get up and to open my laptop literally in bed and to write for as long as I can which is usually three hours maybe that would be a good writing day for me.

When you first started out how did you go about finding an agent?

My best friend is also a writer and he gave my manuscript to an agent without telling me and that person called me and she said I'd like to represent you, and I went to another friend's mother who was also an agent and asked her about it and what she thought of this other agent and she had someone at her agency read it and came back to me and said she wanted to represent me and that was that. I tend to think if you keep working at you're writing and you're writing is good you will eventually find an agent. Don't think that finding an agent process is impossible.

What is your source of inspiration?

It's a combination of things you're always thinking about things, travelling, meeting people it provokes thoughts and also I read a lot of books and I think reading other writers, not just writers, other works of art, so music that I like, films that I like, inspire me. And then I have a few good friends who are writers. Having a community of writers where they are published or not, in my case all my friends are all now published but when we started we weren't, I think that community of people really does keep you inspired and keeps you working through the difficult times.

Do you ever suffer from writer's block?

Every day I suppose, I mean there is no such thing as writer's block. There are just times when you're writing well and there are times when you're writing badly. For me when I'm writing badly I don't stop writing so I wouldn't call it writer's block, it's just not useful writing that I'm producing. Writing is a relationship just like when you're in a relationship it goes through difficult times and really good times and I think we should all expect it.

Do you ever feel inadequate reading other writers work?

I guess totally yes, you think 'oh my God this is so good.' And maybe you do feel a flair of envy and jealousy but you also feel a sense of appreciation. Writers are also readers and when I'm reading, I do wish I could write like that but I wouldn't call it an inadequacy. My goal is not to out-write the other many writers in the world my goal is to write something I myself think is amazing and in that sense inadequacy is more about how far you push yourself.

What do you hope to achieve in your career as a writer?

In terms of what I'd like to achieve as a writer I like to write stuff that to me is politically engaged, aesthetically beautiful that's a standard I myself comply to my work, whether anybody else thinks the same way – those are things I would like to do by writing. Like any other writer I'd like to be recognised in my time for my writing and to make a decent living out of it. At the end of the day I would like to have written some novels that I can say are fantastic in my personal view.

What advice would you give to budding Asian writers?

Don't write for anybody else. Figure out what it is that you want to say for yourself and how you want to say it. Write something that is honest and true to yourself and take it from there because you'll never get back to honesty if you give it up. For me that is the most important thing, to be true to what you believe in as a writer.

And the second thing is I think people sort of self-select when it comes to writing in the sense that being a novelist is a really, really slow process, like an endurance sword so you only really do it if you kind of have to. And part of writing a novel is a test for yourself: How much do you like the idea of being a novelist? And how much of you actually is a novelist? And over the years writing a book that's what you learn.

Many people like the idea of being a novelist but quite honestly couldn't be bothered to spend seven years or however long it takes in which case they're not novelists. Other people keep trugging their way at it, they finish a manuscript but they don't sell it, they try another one and those people are novelists even if they don't get published and I think that is something you have to ask yourself something very honestly. If you write for yourself you're doing something important. Getting published is a matter of good luck and perseverance – and you have to stick with it.

ROOPA FAROOKI

This interview first appeared in The Asian Writer on August 2007

Roopa, what made you write this story?

Bitter Sweets is about the impact of deception on family relationships, and I've always been fascinated by the dynamics of truth-telling within families, a fascination which began from observing how my own extended Pakistani/Bangladeshi family behaved. Like my character Shona, I noticed at an early age that certain things were left unsaid and unexpressed by tacit agreement for the sake of maintaining familial harmony, as though not discussing them somehow made them acceptable. I quickly learned that this moral fog used to cover up awkward or uncomfortable realities was something shared by most families; whether motivated by kindness or convenience, the immediate instinct for many of us is to comfort and conceal with a lie rather than to hurt and expose with the truth. I liked the universal nature of this instinct, and wanted to explore it further in my writing.

Where did the initial idea come from, and how did you develop that into a novel?

I knew that I wanted to tell a story about a family that uses deceit to hold their fragile family structure together across emotional, cultural and geographical divides, to the extent that deception and double lives becomes something of a family tradition, inherited from one generation and passed to the next.

In order to develop this into a novel, I first started working on the character of Henna, the unrepentantly manipulative thirteen year old who deceives her way into a brilliant marriage. Once I knew who Henna was, I was able to work out the sort of person she would marry, the sort of daughter she would have, and who that daughter would fall in love with, and what sort of children she would have in her turn. Once all the family characters had fallen into place, and I was able to start plotting in detail how their deceits would affect their relationships, bringing them together and forcing them apart.

Did you draw inspiration from real life, people you knew, met and worked with?

I think it's impossible not to be inspired by real life and the people whom we meet, and my father's wayward choice of lifestyle (*he was a charming gambler, who found telling the truth rather dull, as though it somehow lacked imagination*) certainly helped me to explore the theme of deception.

With regard to my characters, I didn't want to depict anyone that I actually knew – instead the characters represent different aspects of myself, or the self that I would be if I were a scheming extrovert like Henna, or an unfulfilled romantic like Ricky-Rashid; like most authors, I have drawn heavily upon my own experiences of love and desire, despair and guilt, awkwardness and aspiration in creating them.

Which character did you have the most fun creating and why?

I really enjoyed creating Henna; extrovert and stylish, she is the opposite of what we might expect of a child-bride from a Bengali village sold into marriage – she is very much the mistress of her own fate, and there is something wickedly delightful in how self-serving and self-interested she is.

Which characters did you feel controlled you more than you controlled them?

When I initially plotted Bitter Sweets, the character of Parvez was nothing more than "Shona's Pakistani husband", but when I started writing, he was so appealing that he took on a life of his own, and became a true romantic hero, chivalrous, funny and uncompromisingly adoring.

Did you get attached to writing Bitter Sweets and did you feel satisfied once it was finished?

Writing *Bitter Sweets* was a pure pleasure for me, and I did feel satisfied when it was finished, especially with regard to resolving the tangled lives of my characters. I didn't feel any sense of loss when it was completed, but was really happy to revisit it during the editing and publishing process; it was like meeting up with old friends.

Bitter Sweets has been described as both commercial and literary fiction. Is that the way you intended it to be?

To be honest, when I wrote *Bitter Sweets*, I didn't have an editor or an agent, and wasn't really thinking about its potential market – in the first instance I wrote it for myself, and wanted it to be the kind of book that I enjoy reading. That said I have always wanted my writing to be accessible, but to have a serious emotional core.

Lastly, what have you got lined up for your next book?

I have already written my second novel, which is called *Corner Shop*. It's a family drama with a focus on the symbiotic and awkward parent-child relationship, and is about the unexpected tragedy of fulfilling your dreams too early in life. It'll be out next April, and I hope that the people who liked *Bitter Sweets* will enjoy it.

This interview first appeared in The Asian Writer on August 2007

Why did you feel the urge to write this book, and did you ever imagine at the time that it would be so well received?

I always wanted to write a book, from childhood days – I always had that urge. The trouble when I was younger was not having any material that I was willing to write about. That came years later, developing a willingness to write about my own experiences. It was tragic, because I would take a sensual delight in blank note books and sheets of crisp, unused paper, but I didn't know what to write about. I was really excited when I acquired a word processor in the 1980s, but the firm commitment to write a book was still many years away.

I don't think that I felt comfortable daring to imagine that a book of mine could be so successful and well-received. Such daydreaming seemed self-indulgent somehow, but the daydreams have now come true – I was on 'The Heaven and Earth Show' and 'Midweek', just like I imagined I would be!

How did you feel writing this book? Was it painful to revisit some of the incidents in your past, which you were obviously very uncomfortable with at the time?

I put off writing this book for years, because I assumed that it would be a huge burden of work. I was completely wrong. When I actually sat down to write the book, the process of writing was a wonderful, joyful experience and I really enjoyed the journey. I believe that I have sufficient distance from the experiences that I can now view them somewhat dispassionately. I can still feel each experience, and it is necessary to do so in order to be able to write about them effectively, but the emotions no longer carry any weight. I think this is an aspect of personal growth – to feel an emotion without allowing it to overcome you. And being confident enough to be willing to share it with others.

How did you recall so many of the details so vividly, did you rely just on memory or other techniques?

I have been blessed with an amazing memory for recalling events and details about them. (*Unfortunately, this memory does not apply to useful academic work!*) I used to think that everyone must recall their own life to the same level of detail, but apparently this is not the case.

One thing which helped is that whenever anything significant happened in my life, I felt a part of my mind was already writing about the event, as a detached observer. When I came to actually writing the book, these events were already written about – inside my head – and I just had to type them out.

When we are growing-up, life is a series of school and university years, separated by summer holidays. One big advantage I have is that my birthday is in September, so I was able to write the book as one chapter for every year of my life, with each chapter representing a school or university year. From a structural perspective, this works very well and helps to maintain a natural pace in the book. The book was not written in order and, since I always wrote about whatever I felt like at that time, it was never forced – it was always a pleasure to write.

You originally self-published this book, what was the reason behind this decision?

I self-published because I couldn't get any publisher or literary agent to be interested in taking it on. The few publishers who wrote back all advised me to get an agent. I like to think that JK Rowling helped me to get published and, in a sense, she did. I was on business trip to America in July 2005 (having received all these rejections), and I was in the Barnes & Noble store in Richmond, Virginia – the night that the new *Harry Potter* book was being released at midnight. The atmosphere in the store was really wonderful. It was buzzing with excitement and many people were there in costumes: kids were dressed as Hogwarts pupils; the store manager was a wizard, and so on. I was really enjoying watching all this, so I loitered around in the store, sipping a venti latte from Starbucks. Whilst I was hanging around, I was browsing magazines and I picked up a financial magazine which had an article entitled: 'Ten Things to do With a Thousand Dollars'. One of these things was to self-publish your own book, and the article gave the website address of a self-publishing company owned by Amazon. As soon as I got back to my hotel room, I looked it up and it seemed quite enticing. In fact, it was relatively easy, since all they wanted was the money and the quality of the book was 100% my responsibility. I decided to go ahead.

In September 2005, I received the first batch of my self-published books, and it was also listed on Amazon. At this point, I thought I had arrived, but I had no idea of how difficult it is to market a self-published book. It is very difficult indeed – no-one is interested. But I did get a lucky break. I sent a copy to Scott Pack, the Head Buyer of

Waterstone's, and he wrote back saying that the content was very promising, but the physical book was clearly self-published and not of a good enough quality or price for him to stock in Waterstone's. But he did say that it deserved a proper publisher and he would like to pass it on to a literary agent, if I was willing. This seemed a step backwards to me, since I had already achieved a published book, but fortunately I said 'yes'. The agent called me a couple of days later, having read the book, and wanted to take me on as a client. So self-publishing was the route by which I got an agent and a proper publisher. This journey is described from his perspective by Scott Pack, in an article on my website. The story from his point of view is quite amusing.

Are there any other comments you would like to make on the subject of writing an autobiography and on writing in general that you think would be useful to other budding writers?

From an artistic perspective, you have to want to write and to really enjoy that process. If you don't enjoy writing, and are forcing yourself to do it because you want to write a bestseller (for reasons of fortune and fame), then no-one is going to enjoy reading what you wrote. Your lack of enjoyment will come across in the text.

In terms of writing, you should find your own natural style and also write about what you know about. This might be about your own life, or work experiences, but you have to come across as knowing what you are talking about. The style aspect is very important. If you try to force yourself into a specific style, that will become apparent to the reader and you will lose credibility.

Also, I don't see how you can enjoy the writing if you are deliberately copying someone else's style. It's no good presenting yourself as being 'in the style of Dan Brown', when it clearly isn't your natural style. In terms of being published (if you have met the artistic criteria), you have to believe in the quality of what you wrote. Have your friends read the manuscript and get their honest feedback. Once you are sure about it, find yourself a literary agent. Getting a publisher without an agent is virtually unheard of. It can be a long, hard slog, but you need to persevere. Get a current copy of 'The Writer's Handbook' and follow the instructions which specific agents give about how to present submissions.

As for self-publishing, this should be a last resort if you want wide circulation of your book – but if you are content with only friends, family and colleagues reading it, self-publishing can be an option.

PRIYA BASIL

This interview first appeared in The Asian Writer on August 2007

The characters in the novel, Ishq and Mushq are so life like. Did you draw inspiration from real life or are they entirely made up?

Some of the inspiration is autobiographical – although the intention is not. The journey my characters make from India to East Africa to Great Britain reflects the pattern of my family's migration. There are also a few anecdotes related by family and friends, which I've scattered through the narrative. For example, my grandfather really was caught up, and almost died, in a refugee camp during Partition – exactly like my character, Karam. The latter however, unlike my grandfather, becomes obsessed with history as a result of his experience and restlessly travels the world trying to find an alternative history he can be part of. So, even where the starting point might be fact, fiction gives one the wonderful licence to go wherever imagination bids.

Which bit of the novel did you most enjoy writing?

One of the main characters, Sarna, is a culinary queen. She uses food to express or repress her own feelings as well as manipulate those of others. Indeed, the 'Mushq' in the title is a reference to the smells of Sarna's cooking which pervade the narrative. It was great fun to use food and smell as a recurring motif. As a keen cook myself, I'm very aware of the emotive powers of food and I enjoyed imagining Sarna taking this to the extreme with night-long sweet making marathons to counter the bitter taste of the past, or stuffing the freezer with leftovers for the children who don't turn up to eat the feasts she prepares.

Early on in the novel, OK has a dull moment and is filled with a sense of paralysis as a writer, did you ever feel a loss of hope when writing Ishq and Mushq and how did you overcome this?

Doubt rather than hopelessness was the feeling that most troubled me while I was writing. The constant questioning of whether what you're creating has any value or relevance. When the doubts threatened to overwhelm, I always reminded myself of how much pleasure I got from the act of writing itself. I just focused on trying to write the best novel I possibly could. And also, I kept reading. There's nothing like great fiction to remind you why you want to write.

The ending for me didn't have a sense of closure – perhaps that's because I got too attached to the characters, and wanted to know what happened next. Did you feel a sense of loss or relief when you'd finished the book in its entirety or would you have liked to have gone on?

I knew how the book would finish when I was half way through writing, so – unlike the reader who arrives suddenly at the end to be surprised and moved – I approached it with a sense of inevitability. However much you might want to tie up everything neatly, you realise that characters have their own integrity, which must be respected. Much as I would have liked to force a change of heart and attitude in Sarna, I saw it wouldn't be realistic. Finally, I was satisfied with the end, which, like life, leaves some things resolved, and others open to interpretation. I did introduce an

optimistic note with the birth of a child called Umeed –
Hope. This suggests that things do go on – but it's not for
me to tell that story.

NIKITA LALWANI

This interview first appeared in The Asian Writer on October 2008

Is Gifted a semi-autobiographical novel?

I wasn't a genius, I was introduced to maths at a very basic level, I was introduced to mental arithmetic, juggling numbers, messing about with that sort of maths to have concrete answers. I used to enjoy maths but I never really moved on with it but if I was to focus on maths then maybe it would become a weapon or a chance to be ahead of the game. So it sort of fascinated me in that way, the book is like an alternate history of what could've happened if I had really focussed on maths.

Did your parents encourage you to write and have a career in the Arts? Would they have preferred you to have a more traditional job?

I was encouraged to explore all things, read literature, maths, science, everything. My father used to read lots of Anglo-Indian writing, Russian writing, and seemed to have a lot of books on the shelves that I would read under the covers with a torch. But I decided to become a doctor. My decision to follow a career in Medicine was more to do with my own values of what I could do to make an impact in the world. I always wanted to be a writer, but it didn't fit in with the way I thought I could earn a living. At different stages of my life I never believed it, I think that's part of the immigrant work ethic – you are always thinking how can I survive? How can I be solvent? You never want to go under.

That's ironic given your recent generous donation to the human rights organisation, Liberty – the entire £10,000 prize money from the Desmond Elliot Prize. What made you do this?

I thought the only way I could do that was if I was lucky enough to win an award. I said to my mum when I came home 'cause she stayed with me that night. "I left home with empty pockets and I came home with empty pockets." When you win an award you don't own that money, so you're able to do something with it. You don't own it, two minutes before they announce it, so it's like you never had it. I did feel it was important, and that they are important issues to make a stand on, and I wanted to make a gesture, to give whatever I could. I'm lucky enough to have an advance to keep me afloat to write the next book.

So you're a mother now. How has it changed you as a person?

Motherhood is so much clear and clean joy then I would have known before, I just felt that it's bought such beauty into my life. My daughter was born at the same time as the book was about to be published. She was six days old when the proofs arrived and I was in bed and I opened the proofs and I had this tiny baby, like the size of my hand next to me. It's been a wonderful thing and I have had to learn to reconstruct that mental image of a room of one's own. I rent a shed around the corner and I write there now. I have set hours when I write whether that's the next novel, or journalism, or campaigning stuff that I do. I've just written a piece for an Aids Anthology about Aids in India. I feel that the world has opened up since, I've become more open and self-aware since she's been born.

I read a wonderful piece about your friendship with Stephen Merchant, creator of The Office. Could you tell me a bit more?

We met twelve years ago, we both started out at the BBC together and we were trying to work out who we were and form our identity, like what kind of artists we were? And in terms of being a creative where are you going? I used to get very sucked into my day to day job at Changing Rooms and he was always like 'think of what you want to do and just do it.' He dropped out before me and just started writing *The Office* and got that done. And on one level we've always had this dialogue, but we've always done and written different things. We came together with this interest in adolescent and teen life we always used to discuss that. There's an overlap we always had a lot of discussion about coming of age, finding yourself as a teenager before you get to the adult world.

Was he instrumental when you were writing Gifted?

He's like a good friend with whom there can always be dialogue. During the writing of the novel, when I was writing the final section we'd often meet and just talk about what's legitimate in that experience, what would Rumi do if she wanted to have a boyfriend? It was really basic, trying to work out things, and he was someone to bounce ideas off. Gerard Woodward my mentor was a real help. Whereas Stephen and I are friends, Gerard was my mentor, he was Booker nominated a few years ago and I met him on a creative writing course I would just share work with him and he never really said this is how you write but when I left something would always click. A mentor is someone who makes you a better version of yourself in a way. I think mentors are very important but you could find them in all sorts of ways, they might not be the person you expect. It's very important you hunt them down.

So how did you go about getting Gifted published?

Gifted was bought by Penguin within a matter of days and I'm very grateful for that. I turned up to meet them afterwards and thought, 'Oh my God, they might think you know, here's someone who can't string a sentence together, she can write but she's like a loner and socially awkward, or they might think we didn't want this.'

What advice do you wish you hadn't listened to?

There was plenty but I think I did ignore it, but I wished I'd listened to Stephen more, who used to say, 'don't be influenced by the nitty gritty and the politics around you, if you're going to be intimidated by people, be intimidated by Joyce.'

RANA DASGUPTA

This interview first appeared in The Asian Writer on November 2009

Can you tell our readers, in less than 100 words, what your latest novel, Solo, is about?

It's about a one hundred year-old man who has done almost nothing in his life. It's about trying to make meaning out of failure (it's the opposite of the stories of success, plenitude and achievement that fill our media space) and the enormous reserves of failure that surround every success. It's about war and revolution and friendship, and the eternal inadequacy of words in the face of death. It's about music and chemistry and daydreams. It's about children who are not yet born, and the terrifying beauty of the future.

The blurb of Solo certainly has a wow factor for its refreshingly unique storyline. Where did the idea come from?

Many places, actually. Some parts of the story I'd already worked out many years before I began writing. Little stories people told me or things I saw, that grew over the years into big slabs of this novel. I'd developed this interest in Bulgaria – it was a place that kept prodding me until I sat up and took some notice – and in the end I decided to go there and talk to people and see what it was all about. That's when I found a house to put all these stories into.

What research went into writing the book? Did you travel to Bulgaria and what did you find there?

I read a huge amount about chemistry, Bulgaria, etc. I'm pretty obsessive about the factual parts of my fiction – factual depth makes this kind of writing sparkle more, I find. But the main research involved talking to people. As you can see from the novel, Bulgaria's twentieth century was pretty crazy. Turbulence and violence arrived like floods from the centre of Europe, and Bulgarian lives were turned upside-down. For much of the century, however, it was difficult to talk about these things. Now it is possible to talk about them, which is why Bulgaria is a place of such amazing storytelling. I listened to incredible stories there. It was a privilege to meet the people I met in Sofia.

When you were in the novel writing process did you ever envisage that the story would be talked about, enjoyed and of course hit the bestseller lists like it has?

When I was writing *Solo* I was in the grip of a four-year obsession. I was obsessed with making a perfect thing. It felt rather like sculpture: stepping back to see what you have made and realising it is not working at all, going back to the stone and getting lost in the dust and the sound of the hammer. During that period I didn't really think about how it would circulate once I'd finished it. Once I finished it of course I was interested in what other people would think. But that's a very different kind of thought process, and it's filled with anxiety. Because there's no guarantee that the intensity of your own involvement in something that will be sensed by others. No guarantee that the thing carries with it the enormous obsessive energies that went into making it.

What impact, if any, does great praise from a literary great like Rushdie have on your writing?

I always loved novels from the nineteenth and early twentieth centuries. Reading *Midnight's Children* as a teenager I realised that the novel could still be grandiose and potent in this modern world, and I told myself I would write one, one day. Years later I discovered that Salman had read my work, which was startling in a way I can't describe. But such things, again, are external to the actual process of writing. You write because that is how your particular brand of personality becomes itself – not for other people's praise which, while always lovely, could never be sufficient on its own to drive someone through the crazy enterprise of writing a novel.

Who do you think would enjoy reading Solo and in particular what sort of reader did you have in mind when writing the novel?

I don't know. I think you write with a kind of faith: that things you find beautiful and intoxicating other people might find compelling too. But you don't know who those people will be. Or if they exist. Certainly not how many of them there might be.

Moving away from talking about Solo to your writing journey – did you make a conscious decision to leave the UK for Delhi to write? And if so how do you think that physical journey has changed you as a writer?

I was doing a corporate job in New York when I moved to Delhi. And yes Delhi seemed like a good place to escape to think about writing. New York was impossible – too expensive, too fast, too derisive. It was completely wrong for the journey I was going to embark on, where there needed to be a lot of room to fail, take wrong turnings, start again... What I wasn't prepared for when I came to Delhi was that this was not just a place of refuge, it was a place with a powerful intellectual and creative subculture where many people were trying new things. It was far more nourishing for a new writer than I ever imagined. I've now been in Delhi for nearly a decade and, without me ever intending things to turn out this way, it's become home.

Your writing career began in your late twenties so what influenced you to become a writer at that point in your life?

I guess I had to face up to what was essential and stop doing things because they seemed like a good idea at the time.

So what's next for you as a writer? Another book?

I'm just starting a book, yes. It's a non-fiction work about Delhi. I've been doing a lot of interviews in the city recently, and this has been a new direction in my writing. It's a remarkable moment in this city, and sometimes you have to drop your other plans in order to take stock of your moment. The first part of this work came out in Granta recently and now I'm expanding this into a book.

NIKESH SHUKLA

This interview first appeared in The Asian Writer on October 2010

We've been here several times before discussing your writing. What's happened since we last spoke?

Now, I actually have a book out, *Coconut Unlimited*. It's out in October on Quartet Books. Since we last spoke, I've signed a book deal, started developing a sitcom for a TV channel, eaten my bodyweight in idlis, now I've learnt the recipe, and got rid of a sofa on Freecycle. It's been quite a mad few months. I've also started playing football for the England Writer's Team. Get me.

So tell us a bit more about your forthcoming novel, Coconut Unlimited?

Basically, it's my take on The Inbetweeners. Three Asian kids in an all-white private school decide that they don't fit in with their peers in the playground or at home in their Gujarati community, so to keep it real, set up a hip-hop band called Coconut Unlimited. Except none of them can rap. Much hilarity ensues. We kinda follow a school year in the life of their band as they try to hone their sound, get girls, dodge parents and learn the gangsta rap ways of the streets, all while maintaining their studies. I was really inspired reading 'Sag Harbor' by Colson Whitehead, one of the funniest books ever written. I realised that coming-of-age tales don't have to be about dead bodies in quarries; they can be about whatever you want.

The book's written in first person, how much of it is inspired your life?

A lot. The setting is the one I grew up in, characters are based on amalgamations/mash-ups/constructs of people I knew, small anecdotes that informed my teendom are sprinkled throughout. I tried to walk that line of how when you're teenager, everything is super-important and upsetting and terrifying and amazing no matter how slight it is. The events that spin out of that familiar territory are a different story though. I wanted to base the story in a reality people could identify with and relate to and the most honest way of doing that was to plough and plunder my own school days, my own delusions of grandeur and my mum's incredible hissy fits.

The book's written in an easy to read, conversational style and this gives the reader a feeling that they are very much a fly on the wall of this protagonist's life. What do you think it says about the British Asian experience?

I think it's very true to the push/pull effect kids feel growing up between their environments at home and at school. Which one do you stray towards? Do your choices impact your friend-making-abilities? What happens if you don't commit yourself fully to either environment, you end up lost, like Amit and Anand in the book, meaning that the band becomes the most important thing for them, over being good Indian kids and being cool school chums. I think, what it says about culture and community and how they mutate slowly around us and change is an honest depiction of British Asian life.

And can you explain the word "Coconut" and its implications?

'Coconut' means brown on the outside, white in the middle. It was an insult thrown at kids who weren't desi enough for their desi peers, who appeared to like 'gora' things like Radiohead and beef and the arts. It was a pretty damning thing being called a coconut back in those days. Now (well, up until that recent news story in Bristol), it was thrown around with a bit more abandon. But in the book, these kids are trying to reclaim the word for themselves and question whether it's a bad thing, whether usage of the word is worse than being what it means.

How did you find the process of finding an agent? And how did the publishing deal come about?

I found an agent on the back of the publishing deal. The deal came about when I met Gavin James Bower, my editor at Quartet, through live literature events. He's an author in his own right and liked the book enough to take it to Quartet as an editor. So it all came about through endless readings, and live literature events and short story nights and something eventually gave. Then, once the deal was in place, I started looking for agents, and eventually found one.

So you recorded a song for this too. How do readers access the track?

We actually put together a mixtape for the book. So many rap songs are mentioned in the book and so many lyrics are spat by the protagonists, we thought it'd be fun to record the mixtape they talk about recording in the book. We teamed up with Mr Lingo and Sweatbox Sounds to record it. It contains writers, poets, actors, characters from the book, lyrics and tunes by Wu Tang, Gang Starr, KRS-One, loads more. Lots of the Golden Age of boom bap hip hop I grew up with. I felt that as a debut novelist, I needed to do something extra to help promote the book, and having tried my hand at music in the past, knew a bunch of people I could turn to for help.

Are you still blogging and doing the spoken word nights? How is that going for you now you're a published writer?

Yep, not as much anymore (the blog) and all the time (the nights). I'm doing a bunch of libraries, live literature nights and bookshops in the run up to the book coming out, and then once that's out, I can crack on with book 2, which has been marinating for a while and needs to cook. I find the time to blog harder now because so much creative energy is being poured into the book and getting it out there. It's my first book and I want it to come out right. I do miss blogging about all the stupid stuff I get up to, though and hope to return to the disciplined recording of inane-ness and mirth around me.

What's the weirdest thing that's happened to you since becoming a published writer?

I had a moment the other day when I realised I'd changed. Months ago, I'd complain that no one wanted to publish me and the industry was in a terrible state and no one wanted to take risks. Last week I was complaining about my agent and my publisher taking too long to iron out a minor sub-clause in a contract. That made me think, wow, I'm not in Kansas anymore.

What advice would you give to an aspiring writer?

Read. Read. Read. Write. Write. Write. Persist. Persist. Persist. And repeat. I don't need to go into more detail do I? Find out the writers you like and wanna be like, and read them. Practise your craft, get feedback, learn, and practise more. Keep trying. If it can pay off for an idiot like me with a silly book about rappers, it can pay off for you.

HM NAQVI

This interview first appeared in The Asian Writer on December 2011

When did you realise you were a writer?

I have always had the urge to commit pen to paper – I believe I was three or four when I picked a pen or pencil – and before I could write, before I mastered the alphabet, picked up the Queen's English, I am told that I doodled extensively. I still do.

Homeboy is engaging. It hooks the reader into the story within the first few lines, and keeps a level of anticipation all the way through. Did you have a fire in your belly when you wrote it and how long did it take?

I had a fire in my belly but that fire alone cannot sustain you. Writing, writing a novel, takes Herculean discipline – sitting down day after day after day, come hell, high water, or a death in the family. *Home Boy* took about three, maybe four years to complete. There are times when you can't write – my back gave way halfway through the project – times you won't write, when you have to trick yourself; I developed an elaborate system of rewards, from the promise of a walk around the block water to a cigarette. And I didn't write *War and Peace*.

Is this the first novel you've ever written?

I remember stapling together an anthology of linked stories in class four and presenting them to my teacher. And I understand that linked stories pass for novels these days.

What inspired you to tell this story, about a young Pakistani in the US who finds himself in a very different world after 9/11?

I don't quite remember the genesis of Home Boy – I was at a bar in the Bowery one night, scrawling on the back of a cocktail napkin – but I happened to be in the States at an anxious, unsettled time. I would have written a very different novel had I been elsewhere, Strasbourg, Papua New Guinea, Karachi.

It is often said that a first novel says more about the author. If this is true, what do you think Homeboy *says about you?*

Most debuts are fundamentally bildungsroman. *Home Boy* is grounded in the comic tradition of the American coming-of-age story – *Huckleberry Finn, Goodbye, Columbus, Catcher in the Rye* or *The Mysteries of Pittsburgh,* for that matter. I had to get mine out of the way.

My point being – are you a mummy's boy?

I like to think that I have always been my own man (but you will have to check with my mother).

I recently went to Imran Khan's book launch here in the UK, in which he said, after 9/11 every Muslim became a suspect – what would you say to that?

I am not a political analyst, sociologist or anthropologist. I don't have any empirical data on the matter. I do understand that things were tough, that things in some way remain tough: one came across an exposé in the Associated Press recently, for example, about extensive spying on the Muslim-American community.

What was it like winning the DSC South Asian Literature Prize?

It was fabulous. There were several thousand people in the audience. There were cameras, flashes. But you know, I write because I have to, because I have an itch. Whether I won or lost, I would have to get back to my desk, and write again.

What have you been working on since, is there another book out soon?

I am working on a big, bad comic epic that contends with light and darkness, the universe and its vastness. It's an exciting project, one that keeps me up till six in the morning. And since you ask, I will be done sooner, rather than later.

What advice would you give to an aspiring author?

Become a doctor. The world needs doctors.

Finally what do the initials HM stand for?

I cannot disclose that – I don't know you that well – but I can tell you that V.S. stands for Vidiadhar Surajprasad.

ROSHI FERNANDO

This interview first appeared in The Asian Writer on April 2012

Please tell us a little bit about yourself and how you got into writing?

I am married and have four children. I grew up in London and worked for legal firms in the City until we moved to the Cotswolds about ten years ago. I always wanted to be a writer. My father claimed that I told him I wanted to be a writer when I was three. I don't know if this can be true, but I was a very early reader. About six years ago I decided to commit to writing and started to apply for MAs in creative writing. I was lucky enough to be offered a mentorship sponsored by the Royal Literary Fund with Stevie Davies, a Booker listed author. Stevie is the director of the creative writing programme at University of Swansea, and after I was mentored by her for a year, and wrote my first novel, she offered me a chance to do a PhD with her.

Where did the inspiration for Homesick come from?

The inspiration for *Homesick* was really the individual people whose stories I told. I started with a number of stories that didn't make it into the collection, and then I wrote The Fluorescent Jacket, which trained me in the art of short story. I realised that I had many more stories I felt compelled to write. The idea of calling it *Homesick* came much later, when I realised there was a unifying theme running through all of the stories.

I think I was writing from a position of frustration and perhaps anger – about the rise of the far right and the pandering of consecutive governments to the Daily Mail and its equivalents who fulminate about multiculturalism and do not acknowledge the great good that immigration has done. I wanted to rebalance the arguments.

And where is home for you?

Home is where my husband and children are. We could live anywhere, I think, as long as we're together laughing and eating and hanging out. My children are growing up now, and it's such a precious time, this giving away of these people to the world – I'm making their home more and more safe and welcoming so that no matter where they land, they want to come back to us, even for a little while. Home is food and animals and long walks and each other.

You write about culture and the lives of Sri Lankan immigrants in Britain – what do you hope readers will take away from reading your stories?

I want readers to see the person who runs their corner shop as their equal. A rather posh lady said to me 'I've read your book. It was very interesting to read about people like that.' I said 'I'm 'people like that' actually!' I want to dismiss the idea of race as a class. I want people to see their neighbours as just that.

Where do you write, and do you have a writing ritual or does your writing come in bursts? How do you fit it all in around family life?

I write in an office I have set up in a light lovely room in our house. I am very lucky – but I earned it! I used to write in the darkest room in the house, beavering away like a hermit, and then I realised that your surroundings can really affect the way you write. No writing rituals – I just turn up, day after day, and work until it's done. It's interesting – we can't write unless we live: having a family has made me experience a lot more, challenge myself more. I love writing around them, but have a hand gesture when I am very busy and someone wanders in to ask a stupid question about dinner or their PE kit – if my head is down, but they see my palm facing them like a policeman, they know to retreat quickly. If they don't, normally violence will ensue…

And talking of the form itself – its touted as being the year of the short story this year, why do you think that is? Will you always write short stories?

Bloomsbury have made it the year of the short story – they have brought out five (in my opinion, really strong) collections this year, and Jon McGregor, DW Wilson, Lucy Wood and I are all being reviewed well and having our collections talked about. I hope that on the back of this short stories will be considered as part of the normal reading ritual for most people – as it is in other countries.

I linked my short stories in order to give readers continuity through the book. I took Toni Morrison's advice and wrote the book I wanted to read. I love to read a lead character from another story mentioned in a future story – or in a story from the past, so that the reader has that knowledge of what happened.

I will always write short stories: they are a discipline, and a joy when they come out well. I am writing a novel at the moment, and tackling the larger scale piece is a completely different exercise. I go back to the short story again and again. I love to read them, I love to write them.

Congratulations for recently being shortlisted for the Sunday Times Short Story Award 2011. What were you doing when you got the news and what was the first thing that went through your mind?

It's quite a funny story: we live in the country, so my phone has intermittent signal. They tried to phone and couldn't get through, so texted instead. When I got the text, I was standing in the garden, and I screamed 'Oh my God, I've been shortlisted' but the 'listed' bit didn't come out properly, and everyone thought I'd shouted 'I've been shot' and came running. They have pheasant shoots across the valley, so it could have happened…

How do you know (if you do at all) that what you've written is prize worthy?

You don't know. Writing is subjective. You can make it the best it can possibly be – but eventually, the judge has to understand what you're trying to say, and if it isn't what they want to read, well, then it's not prize worthy. Prizes are a fantastic way to get noticed and are doing an enormous amount for the short story, but all writers have to eventually shrug and say – well, people didn't want to hear from me this time.

Which writers have influenced you most?

SO many! Tolstoy, Shakespeare, William Trevor, Alice Munro, Flannery O'Connor, Toni Morrison.

Finally what are your top tips to producing a winning short story?

Edit and edit and put it away for a while and then edit it more. Pare it down, keep taking things out, don't write up to the word limit, and really love your work – love it and take care of it like it's a child.

SATHNAM SANGHERA

This interview first appeared in The Asian Writer on October 2013

Tell us about your debut novel, Marriage Material and what inspired you to write this story?

I guess the idea came together in 2011, during the riots, which affected Wolverhampton as well as London. I remember watching David Starkey, the historian, on Newsnight, feverishly blaming the riots on "a violent, destructive and nihilistic" black culture, and citing Enoch Powell's 1968 Rivers of Blood Speech, saying that the riots proved that Powell was right about immigration. People sometimes forget that Powell was a Wolverhampton MP, and if you re-read his famous speech you will find that one of Powell's targets was the policy of "integration" which he described as a dangerous delusion, unacceptable even to immigrants such as the Sikhs, who were campaigning at the time for the right to wear turbans and beards while working on Wolverhampton buses. Having done lots of research for my last book into what Wolverhampton was like in 1968, I thought it would be great to write a family story which traced the story of Sikh immigrants from 1968 all the way to the riots of 2011. And Arnold Bennett's 1908 novel, The Old Wives' Tale, which is set in a drapery shop in Stoke, provided a great structure. It is set around one family in a shop in the Midlands between around 1850 and 1910. Mine is set around a family in a Wolverhampton shop between around 1960 and 2012. They are, in the end, very different books, but I would like to think both say something important about Britain.

The story primarily follows three generations of the Bains' family in Wolverhampton and their corner shop. Did you draw on your own family experiences, growing up in Wolverhampton – and how much of you is there in Arjan?

The problem with writing a memoir like my last book, quite an intimate one in my case, is that you end up invading your own privacy. I was very careful about what I said about my family – nothing appeared without their permission. But I didn't think enough about what I revealed about myself. And I probably revealed too much. In a way, writing this new book, a piece of fiction, was a way of changing the subject, to stop people asking me personal questions, or at least have something else to say. But while writing it I realised the questions would never stop – people would continue to think it is about me. So I have tried to be post-modern about it… the narrator seems to be me, but is also obviously inspired by a Bennett character too. At the risk of sounding like of Literature student – I wanted to raise questions about truth, and play a meta-fictional game with it. I hope it works.

I loved your first book, The Boy with a Topknot, which was of course a memoir. How did the writing of Marriage Material differ to your first book and what was the challenges you faced when writing fiction?

Well, the biggest challenge of book one was the emotional trauma associated with the subject matter. It was nice to be free of that! But book two felt quite similar to write, technically speaking, as there is so much fact in it – a lot of research into how shops have changed over 50 odds years, the politics and so on. I see it as historical fiction really, which isn't massively removed from memoir, as a form.

You mention in the acknowledgements that this book is a reworking of Bennett's Old Wives Tale *– how did this come about and was it simply a case of borrowing a good idea and making it your own?*

My friend Lottie Moggach gave me the Penguin Classics edition of this book and the truth is that I never got around to reading it. The appeal of "classics" rather gets knocked out of you when you study English Literature at university. There always seemed to be better things to do than tackle 615 pages by a writer better known for an omelette than for his work. In the end, I read the Kindle edition. And only because I had a long flight to India, it was free to download, and I had run out of other things to read. But it was a revelation to discover that the story, published in 1908 and about the lives of two sisters growing up in a drapery shop in the Potteries, felt more relevant than any of the free newspapers dished out in economy. This is in large part down to the universality of Bennett's themes: in particular, the generation gap (the agony of an older generation watching the rise of the younger); the clash between the provincial and the metropolitan (Bennett contrasts Sophia's life in Paris where she escapes with her lover, with that of her sister Constance in Bursley); and the threat small communities face from industrialisation (his concern about the survival of the small shop echoes now). But I was struck even more by the parallels between the world he describes and my own background as the child of Punjabi immigrants to the West Midlands. Life in the Potteries in Victorian times was hard and dangerous: just as life was for immigrants arriving to toil in Black Country factories in the 1950s and 1960s. Bennett's characters were obsessed with the acquisition of money and social status, in the same way that Punjabi Sikh culture fetishizes wealth over education. Then there is the novel's presiding concern with marriage. Surreally, "Baines", with the vowel dropped, is even a common Sikh surname. Finishing the book in Delhi, it struck me that the structure of *The Old Wives' Tale* could inspire a TV series about a Punjabi family, with the story moved forward a century from (roughly) 1840 to 1905 to (roughly) 1940 to 2005, the setting dragged 34 miles south from the Potteries to the West Midlands, and the characters based in an Asian corner shop instead of a Victorian draper's shop. Not knowing where to begin with a script, this idea gradually morphed into *Marriage Material*. I would love it if my homage inspired people to give Bennett a chance. My book is meant to be a conversation with Bennett… I like the idea of the form echoing the old complaint about immigrants "coming over here and taking over".

It's rare for us as readers to be in the company of a Punjabi family – so much of it is new to me, but also familiar. Why do you think that there is a shortage of books that centre or shed light on Punjabi culture?

Punjabi culture is fundamentally non-literary… or oral. People don't read books much. And education is seen primarily as a way of improving one's employment prospects and making money. But you could say the same about the communities that Bennett was writing about in 1908. And there are many parallels between Punjabi culture and Jewish culture, and Catholic culture… which is good, as a writer you want to aim for the universal.

It's clever and funny writing but you deal with so much, as with your previous work, with really serious issues about race and racism, family and identity as well as independence and inter-dependence as part of those complicated and messy family dynamics with a light touch, but as the same time being careful to be truthful but also with a great deal of compassion. How did you master this sort of writing or is it a case of not over-thinking when writing?

It's not a conscious thing. But I guess a lot of writing coming out of the Midlands, from the likes of Jonathan Coe, Catherine O'Flynn and David Lodge is comic in tendency. A lot of Punjabi products, from Goodness Gracious Me to Bend It Like Beckham, are funny too. And the writers I like most, from Evelyn Waugh to William Boyd have elements of humour.

Your portrayal of modern Asian men is quite damning – you have Arjan on the one hand, who is educated and purposeful but is spineless at times and afraid of his mother. On the flip side you have Ranjit, who is his polar opposite but is a pathetic loser. Do you think this is true reflection of how the Asian man (particularly the second and third generations) is today?

Totally disagree! The thing about human beings is that they are complex, and whatever you say about someone, you can usually say the opposite too. I would say Arjan is those things, but he is also dedicated and thoughtful and has great moral purpose. And as for Ranjit, he is pathetic in some ways, but also charismatic and funny. I like and dislike bits of both of them.

An easier question: Were you at any point tempted to call this book The Boy in a Sweet Shop?

Ha. No. But I did consider calling it: My Mother Was Right. As a lot of my views of marriage have changed over the last decade.

Q. I love the fact that this story centres on the lives of ordinary people in an ordinary place. Do you think you're helping to set a trend among young British Asian writers to write about the places they grew up in, rather than their imagined homelands that have never been home (and are obviously more mysterious and more romanticised than Wolverhampton, Mumbai for example?)

I have no sense of influencing anyone! But I admire writers who write realistically about life, from Arnold Bennett to William Trevor, Junot Diaz, Hari Kunzru and Nikesh Shukla.

Finally what's next for you as a writer?

Not sure. Have an idea for another book, but have one for a script too, and am enjoying journalism massively. Let's see....

PRAJWAL PARAJULY
This interview first appeared in The Asian Writer on March 2014

What inspired you to write your first novel, Land Where I Flee?

I had a two-book deal, and the second book had to be a novel. I'd be lying if I said there I had a story in me that was dying to be told.

As your characters reunite for their grandmother's chaurasi, you can feel the tension mounting and the stress. There are really uncomfortable moments. What were you trying to say about families and the quirks of family life?

You know how it is with family. There are plenty of uncomfortable moments. Often, we don't know what our roles are when two members of the family are at loggerheads with each other – do we intervene, or do we mind our own business? Isn't another family member's business our own? Is it? Where is the line drawn? Encapsulating all that in a novel seemed like a natural thing to do. Uncomfortable silences, rude replies and cold wars take place in every family.

Tell us about Prasanti – she's a colourful character, made for fiction. Where did the inspiration come from to write about hijras?

I think every novelist who grows up in India has a desire to write about eunuchs. They are such fascinating people. They have their own governments, membership rules and hierarchies. I wanted Prasanti to be a eunuch – if there was one aspect of the novel I was sure of even before I started writing the book, it was Prasanti's sexual identity. I wanted to ensure that Prasanti's character didn't come off as a caricature. That'd have been too easy to do.

Ruthwa is a menace. He's cruel and insensitive – nothing like writers I know and interview. Are writers really that difficult?

Ruthwa is aneverywritergonebad. You don't want writers like him around, but you find them everywhere. Egos swollen by the few feature pages dedicated to them and yet frustrated because, of course, more recognition and more money are always better. Some writers are easy, and others are difficult. Ruthwa just happens to be a difficult one.

Your collection of short stories was published to critical acclaim (The Ghurka's Daughter). Now Land Where I Flee is garnering praise worldwide. How was writing a novel different to writing that first book and which did you enjoy more?

I definitely enjoyed writing the novel more than I did the collection of short stories. I started writing a collection of short stories because I thought it'd be easier than writing a novel. I was wrong. A novel gives you plenty of room to play. Of course, part of the reason I found writing the novel easier than I did writing the collection of short stories could be because I had evolved somewhat as a writer between the two books.

There's no shying away from the fact that you've been described as the next big thing in South Asian fiction by various media. What impact, if any, has this had on your creative process and writing?

In the beginning, there was pressure. I then learned that I'd have to learn not to take things written about me too seriously. That's helped. See, you have to learn to laugh at these delightful sobriquets. You take them too seriously, and you're taking life too seriously.

I've not come across many books that draw on Nepali culture before. Why do you think there is a genuine lack of stories in popular culture about the Nepalese?

The stories are there. The writers are there. A few books are being published in South Asia. I think more than anything else it's a matter of publishers in the West needing to wake up to the excellent fiction emerging from the Nepali-speaking world.

What's next for you as a writer – I know you're busy with promoting the book and festivals – are you looking forward to getting back to writing?

Good lord, wouldn't it be wonderful to only write? I realise those days are long gone. My plans keep changing. I have thought of doing a prequel to *Land Where I Flee* or a sequel to each of the stories in *The Ghurka's Daughter*. Then I think of writing a children's book. What do I know? Ha.

RISHI DASTIDAR

This interview first appeared in The Asian Writer on October 2015

Where did your journey of writing poetry begin?

Very atypically, I can pinpoint an exact moment where I had a damascene conversion – where poetry very suddenly entered my life properly, for the first time. Back in about 2008 I was in the big Borders on Oxford Street in London, idly browsing – I'd just got back from a weekend away in Berlin, and was looking for a book, to 'commemorate' the weekend, as it were. I was in that state of drifting, not really concentrating, and I found myself in the poetry section; on display was 'Ashes for Breakfast' by the German poet Durs Grünbein, in a translation by Michael Hofmann. I started flicking through it… and it was like a light going on. I was transfixed – not just by the sheer sensation of, "My God, words can do *this*?" but the sudden sense of "Wow, this is the stuff I want to be writing. Why did no one tell me this existed before?" In my memory, I think I booked myself on an Introduction to writing poetry course at City Lit the day after. There might *actually* have been a few months in between, but hey! that's not as good a story.

Do you remember the first poem you wrote? Was it any good?

Remember it? Not really… oh hang on, I do; it was titled something like 'A scent of you' and was very heavy and leaden – striving to be 'poetic', or rather what I thought of poetic at the time… Suffice to say, I do have it somewhere. I am inveterate hoarder, so everything I've ever written lives in some shape or form on a memory stick or under my desk at home. But no, I'm not going to go and look it up to see how bad it was.

Tell us more about how you developed your creativity as a poet, and what resources were fundamental to the process?

It sounds a little trite to say it, but it really was and is as simple as reading the work of other poets. It's only through doing that do you start to discover: what you like, what you don't like, who you want to emulate, who you want to rip off, who drives you wild with envy, whose work you think, well I reckon I can do better than that... It's an under-discussed process this, trying to locate yourself in relation to other writers, and trying to find the space in which your voice, your obsessions can then start to take root and make sense. It takes time, and only happens by ranging widely in what you read. In terms of resources to help do that, I'm fortunate in that my day job means that I can afford to spend lots of weekends shopping in a bookshop of some description; and I'm also fortunate to live close by the Poetry Library at the Southbank Centre in London, where I'll have a deep dive into poetry magazines from time to time. But, and forgive me for sounding modish, I guess over the last few years, it's through social media that I've discovered the poems and poets that I've wanted to spend more time with. Thoroughly modern, and very difficult to systemize – but it's also heartening to know that, however little attention the rest of the world might give to it, it doesn't take much effort on Twitter and Facebook to discover thriving communities of people talking, thinking, writing and loving poetry.

Do you have a favourite collection of works that you find yourself going back to, time and time again?

Well, definitely the aforementioned 'Ashes for Breakfast'; that's the thing that's like a clean blast of water to my head; it revives me, gets me started again, particularly when writing isn't going so well; when I have lots of starts, but the poems aren't necessarily cohering into something – anything. What else… Frank O'Hara's 'Lunch Poems' is well thumbed, as I love his approach, his attitude to life – and it fits into your pocket. And I always try to read Vikram Seth's 'The Golden Gate' once a year. I love how it freewheels across the dream of California living and Silicon Valley, the way it dazzles with its virtuosity and phrase-making. And I am in love with that form – Onegin sonnets in tetrameter are something I try to write to kick-start myself out of rut.

Who would you say has had the most influence on your writing life and why?

Two places / institutions in particular. I was very fortunate to study at the Faber Academy in 2010/11 under Jo Shapcott and Daljit Nagra. To call it a six-month long masterclass would be to understate how revelatory and amazing it was. It was just a wonderful period of reading loads, being introduced to new names, challenged every week to write new things, take risks and be daring with your voice, and all in the company of wonderfully talented fellow students.

The other was The Complete Works II, the Arts Council initiative designed to find and support advanced Black and

Asian poets in the UK. I think being selected for that is the closest I'm ever going to get to winning a lottery ticket in my life. Almost every moment of that was a wondrous revelation, and I often had to pinch myself that I was lucky enough to be getting all these incredible experiences – mentoring from Daljit; being on a course at an Arvon Centre and tutored by Catherine Smith and Mimi Khalvati; being in the same room as Warsan Shire wrote and then read a first draft of a poem; reading at the Southbank Centre…

And it wasn't just at the level of craft. Over the course of the programme, I started to think much about not just writing, but what it means to be a writer – maybe even an artist – and the responsibilities that come with that, especially political ones. It woke me up to the fact that, coming from the background I do, it can never just be about *writing* – there are other issues you have to be aware of, deal with, even if it doesn't surface directly in your work.

Can you tell us more about the creative process of writing a poem? What approach do you take? Is there an inspired moment?

So, let's talk about the poem I've given you to go with this interview. I've been carrying around what has ended up the title for well over a year now – the phrase has been hanging about on a piece of paper, and then a notebook, and coming with me everywhere. And then about two Saturday's ago, I woke up with the image that has become the last line – and I knew that the two would go together in some way. The remaining three lines? Well, they started with me playing a White Stripes song last Sunday, and let's say I borrowed a sentiment from a lyric in it… and the rest of it rolled out from there. Since then I've been taking words out, putting them back in, right up until having to send it across, and I'll probably keep playing with it for a while yet… poems oscillate: they suggest they're ready, then you look at them six months later and it's blindingly obvious what needs to change.

That's a relatively typical for how a poem comes about for me. I've very much driven by a phrase, some construction or combination of words that is oddly appealing in some way, and then I have to wait for the bigger ideas that help to fill it out. I'm not great at picking a subject and saying, "Hey, now I'm going to write about this." I've never been the sort of writer that has a big message for the world. That said, I've found myself writing some more obviously political poems recently – but even then, there will be some oddity of speech or phraseology that sparks it off. The trick is then finding that balance of sound and music and language and ideas and form.

Simple, when I break it down like that.

What would you say, is the most challenging part for you, when writing a poem?

Starting… finishing… rewriting in between… it's all, how shall we say, not easy. I have to steel myself against a glib fluency that doesn't mean that much. Ultimately, what I have to fight against is the sense that I've written something just for the sake of writing something – move away from the poem being a bit of idle practice, and think much more about: why does this poem exist? What makes it urgent? Is it just a fancy bit of language (not that there's anything wrong with that but…) or am I actually getting at some deeper, bigger truth – does it matter? Answering that satisfactorily – or at least enough that you're willing enough to let the thing out into the world – knowing which side of that line a piece lies, that's hard.

You're part of the editor development programme at Rialto, can you tell us more about that and how it's helped develop your own poetry?

Well, I should say the programme has actually finished now. Me and Holly Hopkins, the other person on the programme, we 'graduated' with the publication of issue 83 of The Rialto a few months ago. The programme was a fab chance to work at the elbow of Mike Mackmin, the editor of The Rialto, to see up close how a poetry magazine is put together, and to start to get to grips with the folders of poems that arrive – and then to try and exercise some judgement as to what poems we found exciting enough to want to put into the magazine. It was a rapid, in-depth education in working out how and why a poem might 'work', and then – almost as importantly – whether it's right for the magazine too. I learnt a lot about the dedication that it needs and takes to put something out every couple of months – and by extension, that most of the poetry world runs on that dedication.

Has it affected my poetry? I'm not sure that it has – I think it's reasonable to say that, in terms of style especially, I didn't see any submissions that made me think, 'Cor there's someone writing a bit like me!' I hasten to add that that fact hasn't made me think that I should change my style… What looking at all those poems did confirm is that I have to make sure my drafts are as tight and as 'finished' as possible before being sent out: giving your poems the best chance of succeeding, basically.

What do you look for, from an editor's point view, in a poem? How can you tell a poem works?

I think this is the hardest thing of all to be able answer succinctly. It's not enough to say, 'You just can' – but equally the poems that *do* work are so perfectly formed they give you almost no space in which to actually be able to deconstruct them to illuminate them further; the trick of perfection, I suppose. I can best summarise it by suggesting that when you read something that works, you're struck very early on by the sense that, yes, there's a performance here that's starting to come together; you're then in the position of willing the thing to succeed. I guess akin to a tightrope walker: whether you like the person or not, once they get halfway across all you want is for them not to fall off.

There are technical things you learn to start to look for: has a rhyme scheme started been followed through – and if not, is it ok that it doesn't? Is the meter held all the way to the end? Has an idea that's been sketched out fully realised? Are the metaphors and / or similes vivid, interesting – new? Again, it's hard to systemize – this stuff is never done on a checklist – but by reading more, you're able to gauge much more easily what's good and what's bad.

What advice would you give to a poet who's just started writing?

Read, read, read, read; oh and read. If you want to get good at the writing of poetry there is no other way than spending lots of time immersed in poems, and poetry. It's not that you have to like everything that crosses your desk and screen – but it is so much easier to do now, especially as the internet means that single poems float freely towards you, without you having to look and search that hard. Read the old stuff certainly – but read new too. We're lucky in that, right now, there are so many new names and talents who are emerging, producing interesting, stimulating and dynamic work. If you don't know where to start, you can head to the Poetry Library, settle down with a few magazines (naturally I recommend The Rialto) and you'll rapidly find stuff that will get you thinking, move you – and then go on from there. Lots of unread volumes aren't a challenge to be tackled; they're a pleasure waiting to happen.

Do you think it's becoming easier for Black and Asian poets to find outlets to publish their work? Is there a collection in the pipeline that we can look forward to?

Well, the second part of that is easier to answer: I'm working on *something*, and hopefully that will emerge soon; watch this space…

As to the first; I think it is, yes, but probably not as fast as it could or should. That isn't to denigrate the efforts of many editors and publishers who I do know spend a lot of time aiming to make sure that they have a good spread, balance of BAME writers to feature. But thanks to the success of programmes like The Complete Works, we've now got a situation in which people are far more aware that an absence of non-white poets looks, at the very least, odd in a multicultural society. And we're seeing much more activity around changing that situation, so that's positive.

But don't forget, this is a two-way process, and it relies on BAME writers to get out there, start writing, start sending, being persistent. If you're not in the submission folders, you've got no chance of being seen, being published. The point is: you cannot be shy. You have to work, yes – to get good, better at your craft, continually. You need to participate, give back to the poetry world – you can't just sit scribbling, and hope for your genius to be discovered. Go to readings, support your fellow poets, listen hard to their words, buy their books, subscribe to magazines; join your local writing group, give your feedback to their poems kindly and generously… love the world that you're starting to enter, basically. And you'll see that with time and persistence, a bit of luck, the doors that you're knocking on will start to open. I mean, I didn't think they would for me – but they're starting to now.

And even if they didn't, it doesn't actually matter anyway. I'm still going to be writing those Onegin sonnets, for me, well into my dotage; this is a vocation now. So I'm going to keep writing whether the world cares for my words or not.

SUNJEEV SAHOTA

This interview first appeared in The Asian Writer on October 2015

You've had a great year. Congratulations! Did it feel good from a writing perspective, or was it distracting?

It felt good. My work got into the hands of more readers than it would have done otherwise – that's a wonderful feeling. But, it's true: I've written nary *(a regional word for 'not')* a word for six months.

What's the best book you've read this year?

I thought Mrs. Engels by Gavin McCrea was pretty marvellous.

You're one of very few writers who don't have an online presence. You aren't on Twitter, Facebook and you don't have your own website (or one we could find). Do you think this activity can be distracting, especially for a young writer, such as yourself, who is still learning the craft?

It's just not a world I have much interest in, and neither do I see how having a presence online is going to make a (net) positive impact on my work. To be honest, I find saying what I really mean hard enough – and excruciating enough – in a 5,000 word essay, let alone 140 characters.

I read that you're making space in your basement to write. Are you trying your best to shut out the world and what can a writer gain from doing so?

I have two kids and the basement is the only place I can make into a study, away from the noise of family life. I'm incredibly easily distracted (another reason for me to avoid social media) so find I need solitude to spur my writing, and reading for that matter.

Tell us about your writing ritual. When are you most productive?

When in the thick of a first draft I write from 10am to 2pm on Tuesdays and Wednesdays. Thursday is my full writing day. I'll try and do a bit on Fridays and Saturdays as well, if life allows, which it generally doesn't.

You didn't read a novel til you were 18 (I remember this from our first interview!) What do you think we could do to encourage more boys, in particular, to read fiction?

Boys do read fiction, or, at least, they do until they start being made to feel they're not very good at it. I'd let boys read whatever they want – gaming zines, graffiti apps, gangsta poetry, whatever – and stop making them feel like those forms don't have literary value. Of course, boys, along with everyone else, need somewhere to go to get their books, so shutting down libraries is a tremendously stupid thing for any government to be doing.

Diversity has been talked about so much this year in publishing from #WeNeedDiverseBooks to #DiverseDecember trending on Twitter and Spread the Word's damning report on the marginalisation of BME writers. There's been a huge push to encourage people to read books by writers from BME backgrounds and for publishers to publish them. As one of Granta's best young British novelists and one of few BME writers to have been shortlisted for the Man Booker Prize what your thoughts on the subject?

The diversity debate seems to go on and on without ever actually getting anywhere; it's like the publishing industry's Zeno's Paradox. One thing: prizes are, perhaps unfortunately, tremendously important to our literary culture and, for me, any prize list that isn't diverse isn't a list that's worth any reader's time: the judges, shamefully, haven't done a good enough job of looking beyond their own face.

Both your books, Ours are the Streets and The Year of the Runaways have been based in Yorkshire, where you live. Do you feel some responsibility to share stories that might not otherwise get written about in places that aren't wholly represented in fiction?

I only write the stories that interest me; writing a novel takes too long to spend it doing anything else. If it looks like I'm sharing stories that might not otherwise get written, then that's probably a function of the sad fact that there are so few published writers from the British-Sikh community.

What has your personal experience been of the publishing industry? If you could change one thing what would it be?

So far, hugely positive. I've been very lucky – my agent, editor and publicist are all talented, amazing people who understand my work and my vision for it. What would I change? I'd bring back the Net Book Agreement.

What are your writing goals for 2016?

To make a start on the next novel, and maybe even get a first draft of the first half down.

ABIR MUKHERJEE

This interview first appeared in The Asian Writer on June 2016

As a qualified accountant you came into writing later in life. Tell us more about how and why you decided to become a writer?

My journey from accountant to writer began back in the autumn of 2013. I was thirty-nine at the time, hurtling towards forty and I had the hope that maybe there might be more to life than accounting.

I'd always wanted to write a book but never had the confidence. Then one morning I saw an interview with Lee Child where he talked about how, at the age of forty, he started writing, and I thought why not? I'd never read any of his books till then, but I went out that day and bought a copy of his first book, Killing Floor, and devoured it within forty-eight hours. I was amazed at how simply written and well plotted it was. I'd recently had an idea for a story centred on a British detective who travels to India after the First World War, and reading Killing Floor gave me the motivation to put pen to paper.

Nevertheless, I'd have probably given up after about ten thousand words if it weren't for a piece of good fortune. I'd been doing some research online and came across details of the Telegraph-Harvill Secker Crime Writing Competition, looking for new and unpublished crime writers. The entry requirements were simple: the first five thousand words of a novel, together with a two-page synopsis of the rest of the book. There was only one stipulation – that the entry contained some international element. I tidied up the first chapter, wrote the synopsis and sent them away.

Having never submitted anything before, I didn't expect to win, so it was a complete surprise when, a few months later, I was contacted by Alison Hennessey, the organizer of the competition, and told that my book was going to be published. The problem was at that point I didn't have a book, just half a first draft of fifty thousand words that didn't always fit together. Thankfully Alison and the whole team at Harvill Secker took me under their wing and helped me turn those fifty thousand words into a fully-fledged novel.

When do you find the time to write?

To be honest, it's not easy finding the time. I still work full time and have a wife and two young children, which means writing has to take a back seat to work pressures and family time. Luckily, my wife, Sonal, is very understanding, and helps me to make the time. Generally I end up writing at weekends or late at night, though I tend to be thinking of plots and stories almost all of the time.

What impact did winning the Telegraph Harvill Secker crime writing competition have on your writing?

It had a huge impact. I was a complete novice to the world of writing. All of a sudden I had a book deal and more importantly an editor, an agent and a whole team of people at Harvill Secker guiding me. To be honest, what with the pressures of work and family life, I'm not sure I would have had the confidence or the determination to keep writing without the support that came with winning the competition.

A Rising Man is your debut novel, tell us a little about the inspiration behind the story?

The story follows Sam Wyndham, an English detective who comes to Calcutta after the Great War in search of a new start. He's immediately thrown into his first case, the murder of a British *burra sahib* who's been found with his throat cut in an alley. Sam, aided by his Indian assistant Sergeant Banerjee, investigate and soon find that things are a bit more complicated than they expect.

Really though, the book is about the different cultures in India during the period and the impact of colonialism on both the rulers and the ruled. In particular I wanted to understand what happens when a democratic nation subjugates another, both in terms of the impact on the subjugated peoples, but just as importantly, on the psyche of the people doing the oppressing. I think the moral and psychological pressures placed on those tasked with administering the colonial system were immense and it's something that's been relatively unexamined.

I've always been interested in the period of British Rule in India. I think that period in history has contributed so much to modern India and to modern Britain, but it's a period that's been largely forgotten or mischaracterized, either romanticised or brushed under the carpet.

I've always been rather surprised by this and wanted to look at it from the point of view of an outsider who's new to it all. One of the things that has always fascinated me is that, in an era when totalitarian regimes were rampant in Europe, regularly murdering anyone who showed any dissent, in India, this largely peaceful freedom struggle was playing out between Indians and their British overlords. At the time, there was no parallel to this anywhere in the world, and I think it says a lot about the people of both nations, that such a struggle could be played out in a comparatively civilised way.

We're in 1920's Calcutta. What research did you do around the period to ensure historical accuracy? Were there instances where you were happy to forego these in favour of fiction?

Historical accuracy was very important to me in terms of the sort of messages I wanted to get across, and that meant quite a lot of research. My parents are both from Calcutta so there was a lot of asking of questions of old family members and friends. I also made a few trips to the city and that helped me get a sense of the place. During one visit, I was lucky enough to be given access to the Calcutta Police Museum where a lot of the police documents from the period are on exhibit. That was fascinating, as the Kolkata Police today has a rather ambivalent view of its own history during that time.

At the same time though, a lot of research was done sitting at home and trawling the internet. It's amazing what you can find out these days by just Googling! There was however one particular area where I had to forego historical accuracy. The novel is set during the week of the Jallianwalah Bagh massacre and in reality, the news of the massacre was suppressed and took several weeks to filter through to Calcutta and other Indian cities. For the purposes of the plot, I couldn't wait for that to happen so I altered things so that news of the atrocity reaches Bengal the morning after.

Your main character is an English detective in Calcutta. I was grateful for the humour this allowed for. Was it important for you to include lighter moments in a crime novel?

I think so. My main character, Sam, has just survived the Great War. He's been traumatised by it and by the loss of his wife. He's come to India and he sees that many of the things that he thought he was fighting for such as liberty and self-determination are actively withheld from Indians. His way of dealing with the hypocrisy and absurdity of it all is to employ a rather wry, gallows humour.

As I read I felt like I was transported to a different place and time but I also loved the explanations which helped to guide me. Who do you write for? Is it the generation that have grown up without really knowing their 'homeland' or is it another audience entirely?

That's a very good question. On one level, I'm writing for anyone who likes a good crime thriller, but on another, I'm writing to highlight aspects of our history that have been forgotten or mischaracterized. To that end I'm writing for everyone who is interested in that shared history between Britain and India. Of course, first and foremost that includes British-Asians like myself, but also, I'd hope it would be interesting to white British people and people further afield.

You've mentioned before that you have a love and fascination for Calcutta. What is it about Calcutta that inspires you to set your work there?

In the period that the book is set, Calcutta was still the premier city in Asia and was as glamorous and exotic a location as anywhere in the world. At the same time, it was a city undergoing immense change and was the centre of the freedom movement, a hotbed of agitation against British rule. It seemed the natural choice for the series I wanted to write.

How did you find the publishing journey and working with an editor to revise your manuscript?

I found the publishing journey to be a fascinating experience. I'd never really written fiction before so the whole thing was a very steep learning curve. Fortunately my editor was fantastic, and guided me through the whole process, from first draft to final, published book. It was a process that lasted about two years, but from day one, I took the decision that I would follow all the advice I received, whether I agreed with it or not, simply because I was new to the whole thing and my editor was one of the best in the business. It's was definitely the correct decision and as the process went on and I learned more, I found myself agreeing with pretty much everything she'd suggested.

Will Captain Sam Wyndham be returning for another installment and if so, how far along are you with writing the next book?

Most definitely! Part of my objective has always been to look at the whole period between 1919 and Indian independence through the eyes of Sam and his Indian assistant Sergeant Banerjee. I'm hard at work on book two, which is partly set in one of the Indian princely states and this should be out next May.

KAMILA SHAMSIE

This interview first appeared in The Asian Writer on October 2017

Where did the inspiration for Home Fire, and to write a contemporary version of Sophocles Antigone, come from?

The inspiration came entirely from Jatinder Verma who runs the Tara Arts theatre in London. He suggested that I might adapt Antigone in a contemporary context as a play. Once I started to think about it though, I realised there was a novel in it, set in contemporary London (and perhaps I also realised that my brain doesn't really know how to write plays).

Your story starts with Isma being interrogated at the airport having to prove her British-ness. What did you want to say about the challenges of being British and Muslim in Britain today?

I don't ever write novels because there's something I want to say. I write novels to explore characters and ideas – having become a British citizen in 2013 I was particularly interested in how citizenship laws change, and what they reveal about a country. In particular, I was interested in Theresa May (who was Home Secretary at the time) wanting to expand the laws to strip people of citizenship, and the ways in which that was clearly aimed particularly at British Muslims.

What would your Google search reveal about you?

I can't possibly answer that question with total honesty.

Both Isma and Aneeka choose to wear some sort of head-covering but this isn't central to their character necessarily. Why was it important for you to make this distinction and for them to be practising Muslims?

Do you know anyone who views a hijab as central to their character? I don't. It's often central to how other people view women in hijab, but that's a completely different matter. Many of the decisions that happen in a novel aren't thought through ideas – they're just part of the way character and story unfold as you write. When I first started to write Isma's character I didn't imagine her with her head covered, but about one page in I found myself writing something that indicated she does cover her head, and I thought, well, ok.

I tend not to question these early decisions in the writing process -you just go with them and see where they lead.

I chuckled at Aunty Naseem's 'In my days either you were the kind of girl who covered your head or you were the kind of girl who wore make-up. Now everyone is everything at the same time.' What has surprised you most about Muslim female identity and how it has changed over the past decade?

I don't think anything has particularly surprised me, but perhaps I say that because I don't feel 'Muslim female identity' is something I particularly have a view on. Just in the last year or so I've been in Sarajevo, Istanbul, Karachi, London, New York – all places where I've encountered many Muslim women, but I don't think there's anything in particular I can say that would bind them all together under the term 'Muslim female identity'. I would guess that broadly speaking, Muslim women in Sarajevo have more in common with their non-Muslim compatriots than they do with Muslim women from Pakistan or Turkey.

Where were you when you received the news that Home Fire was longlisted for the Man Booker Prize? How did you react?

I was in a supermarket, buying rice. I reacted by putting down the rice and walking out of the supermarket in order to call my parents and sister.

Many of your characters in Home Fire appear to have a misguided relationship with religion. What are your thoughts on religion and its purpose in modern society? Would you say Islam is compatible with the West?

I don't think it serves any purpose to even ask the absurd 'is Islam compatible with the West' question.

As for my characters – I don't actually see many of them as having a misguided relationship with religion. Certainly, the young man Parvaiz is misguided by an older man who uses a certain kind of religious rhetoric to brainwash Parvaiz, but religion actually has a very minor role in the brainwashing. And there's a man who was once a practising Muslim and is now an atheist but I would call that a non-relationship rather than a misguided relationship with religion.

As for religion's purpose – it's always been a force that can be used to either give people strength or to constrict them, it's always been a force that can be used to make people behave more generously or more viciously. Modernity hasn't changed any of that. Of course how religion interacts with those who are followers of other or of no religion is a question that's very important, as is the question of how religion adapts itself to new contexts – but none of these are new issues.

In our current political times would you say it's more important than ever, that writers also take on the role of activist?

No. Activists know how to be activists; novelists know how to be novelists. That doesn't mean writers don't engage with the world around them – I just don't think activism is necessarily the way in which they do it. And I do think we'll be seeing more politically engaged novels coming out of the UK in the years to come.

This is your seventh novel. What have you learnt most about yourself through writing?

That I'm far more interested in answering questions about characters I make up than I am in answering questions about myself.

Finally what's the best and worst advice you've heard (or listened to) on writing?

Best advice – know the rules of writing, understand the rules of writing, but don't forget the only real rule is 'if it works, do it'.

Worst advice – can't think of any. If it strikes me as bad advice I suppose my brain doesn't retain it.

MEENA KANDASAMY
*This interview first appeared in The Asian Writer on December
2017*

When did you decide that this story needed to be written?

There are two moments that are crucial: there was one point
within my marriage when I knew that I had to write out what
I was living through because it seemed so improbable,
incredible and horrendous and above all, frightening. I knew
that to write this story was going to be my way to write
myself out of that story—almost as an escape. In that sense,
the decision to write it came when I was inside the marriage,
and because I had made this mental commitment that I
would tell this as a story to the outside world, I also made a
promise to myself to live accordingly—as a strong woman, as
someone who could endure things so that she could
eventually emerge unscathed. When you live life as a writer,
I think writing feeds your life as much as your lived
experiences feed your writing. I remember very clearly the
moment when I actually started writing this novel. I was
with my writer-friend Pilar Quintana, we were both on a
residency in Hong Kong in 2012—and we had both walked
out of marriages that we did not want to remember. We'd
hunt down all these little cafes were smoking was still
permitted and go and sit there and try to write. Pilar wrote
on a computer, I just wore cheap and fancy sunglasses and
pretended to write. I carried a thin red A5 notebook with
me, in which I would record some fragment or the other, in
a very, very stylized register and hope that eventually
everything would make sense.

Why did you choose to tell the story using fiction rather than non-fiction?

To me, the divide between fiction/non-fiction is a marketing thing. So much of fiction is real, and so much of non-fiction (the memoirs of politicians) are huge, glossy, ghost-written lies. The truth value–the more you lay a claim to it, the more others are going to dispute it. So it is best to leave it at the doorstep and get ahead with telling the story you want to say. The pertinent question would be: why a novel instead of a memoir–and I chose a novel because of its ability to hold literally anything, because of its flexibility, because it allows you a certain license.

I think it's really important that your protagonist isn't a subservient housewife. She's an educated, middle class activist. And yet she finds herself in this abusive marriage. Was it important for you to dispel the notion that domestic violence only happens to a certain kind of woman?

Yes. The can of worms that the #MeToo campaign has opened up has shown that women are victimized and sexually preyed upon irrespective of the profession which they enter. I think it's the same with domestic violence–you can be illiterate and beaten up because a man assumes he can discipline you; you can be a PhD and beaten up because he thinks that he's delivering blows to your arrogance by being physical with you. Brute force does not look at which women is at the receiving end, just the same way in which brute force does not look in the mirror. There is no single prototype of victim, just as there is no single prototype of perpetrator.

Is it important for us as readers to be uncomfortable to learn certain truths? Stories of sexual assault and harassment have dominated headlines in recent weeks, and a #MeToo campaign on Twitter has highlighted the extent of the problem. Are you hopeful things will change as a result of these revelations?

Yes–I think squeamishness, taboo, politeness have all evolved in society for a variety of reasons but sometimes they can be double-edged swords–not allowing us to confront the demons that exist in our midst. So, yes, violence, rape, stigma–these are not easy things to talk about–but we need to have that conversation, sooner than later, before these things turn deadly. I personally believe that putting things out in the open, calling out oppression for what it is, and for the damage that it inflicts on women is crucial and necessary–and in the end, will certainly benefit women.

In the novel, your protagonist types words for herself without ever saving the document. Through the act of writing she feels stronger, and reclaims a sense of self. What do you make of writing as a form of self-help?

To me–writing this novel is not self-help. I've been through traumatic and painful episodes in the past–and the easiest and best response to me has been going on with life as if nothing has happened. I've learnt that the hard way, and I've perfected it to an art–and I think it's a great coping mechanism. For me, writing is something else. There's this implicit dualism where as a person I want to forget all the bad shite and move on, where I want to live gloriously as if nothing has ever hurt me–and then as a writer–I want to go over the wounds, open them up, let them bleed. Not just in this story of a violent marriage–but that is how I'm in general. Within a circle of friends, in social gatherings, I'd perhaps be the most chilled out person–and then when I write I try to be incisive and surgical. I think of that as compartmentalization. We need to forget and pretend nothing has happened to get over with the everyday–but we also owe it (not just to ourselves, but to society) to unmask and peel away the layers of social hypocrisy and cultures of violence.

How has writing this book affected your relationships with family and friends if at all?

No. And I'm not the type of person who would every write something that would wound anyone I love, or have ever loved. Which is why the liberty of the genre of a novel, and its implicit air of fictionality allow me to shelter precious people in my silences.

Finally what advice would you give to a writer who is writing experimental fiction?

I don't know. For me, experimental fiction became the default because I was telling stories that are not easily told–stories where the workshop-novel, or the template-novel would be bound to fail because so much had to be told. Anything I do–fall (and stay) in love, write, read–is something to defeat boredom–so I could never ever write something staid and sedate. I would give it up.

MEET THE AGENT: Lorella Belli
This interview first appeared in The Asian Writer on July 2008

Could you please tell our readers a little bit about yourself and how you became a literary agent?

As long as I can remember I have always been passionate about books and people, so I knew my ideal job would have to deal with both. Book publishing was the perfect industry for me, and when I discovered the role of literary agent, I knew straight away that's what I wanted to be. I guess what appealed to me was the opportunity to discover and promote new writers, and to sell their work to publishers and other media. I love the fact that I can combine the editorial side of things with the deal making, the contract negotiations, as well as the networking and social aspect of it. To me it's a lifestyle, a way of living, not just a job, because you can and do get ideas or meet potential authors everywhere, you never stop really. It's definitely not a 9-to-5 job, it's hard work but incredibly rewarding – nothing beats calling an author to tell her/him we have just received an offer for their book (especially if it's a nice large one!), and listening to their reaction and satisfaction when they realise they are about to achieve their dream.

I have worked in publishing for twelve years for various publishers and literary agencies before setting up my own agency in London's Notting Hill in 2002. I studied in Venice and my MA dissertation was entitled "The Literary Agent as Businessman and as Promoter of Literature'. We are members of the Association of Authors' Agents and I am often asked to give talks to creative writing courses students, writers' groups and at literary festivals. I also teach a seminar on how to get published at the Portobello Business Centre, London (*for more information, please contact the agency*) and am an Ambassador for the Girls, Make Your Mark! A nationwide campaign which aims to kick-start a more enterprising culture amongst young people in the UK, especially women.

What does a literary agent actually do?

Agents sell third parties (for example book publishers) the right to produce market and publish books, not the books themselves. To put it more simply, we sell various types of rights in the intellectual property created by our writers, and we manage their career.

I'd say agents tend to have two main functions for authors: business and personal (career advice, encouragement, stability, support, even friendship)

On the business front, what agents can offer authors include editorial feedback; this is a key function especially nowadays when editorial departments are overworked and you need to submit to publishers' material that requires little work in most cases. However, bear in mind that the agent's editorial input is not copy editing, the agent will be considering the big picture when assessing your work (overall value of book, structure, characterisation, dialogue, readability, and basic talent, etc.)

An agent would then submitting an author's work to a publisher/newspaper/producer, etc., that is matching the project with buyer; looking for best possible publisher or editor for your book; and negotiating and getting best possible terms for authors (in terms of advance, royalty percentage, split of subsidiary rights, promotional effort, and general interest in the book); drafting and negotiating contracts; selling other secondary rights not granted to the publisher (for example, translation, audio, dramatic, etc.) The agent will also be responsible for collecting the money due, checking (and querying if necessary) royalty statements which publishers prepare twice a year (showing sales and profit/loss); for getting feedback from publishers (sales figures, print runs, marketing plans, etc.) for reverting rights to the author if a license has expired; in general promotion of author at every opportunity, attending book fairs etc.

In short, if you have an agent, she/he is your closest ally in publishing. You'll have someone fighting for you all the way, supporting you and sharing and enjoying your success with you.

What are the benefits of using a literary agent as opposed to contacting a publisher directly?

There are a number of benefits to the author, in terms of the income that can be earned and the control over their work authors can have for example.

One should bear in mind that while the editor is paid by the publisher, the agent is paid by the author. The agent gets a percentage of whatever money they make for the author, so their interests coincide and their incomes are directly linked. It is not the same for your publisher, who will of course benefit if your book does well, but should this not be the case, she/he can still rely on other books and is paid no matter how they perform.

Also the agent's commission charged tends to be much lower than the percentage a publisher would charge an unagented author for the sales of the same sub rights. For example if you have an agent and your agent managed to keep serial rights in your book, she could sell your book for serialization to a newspaper before publication and any money from such deal (minus the agent's 15%) comes straight to you, that is you get 85% of the amounts received from the paper. On the other hand, if you don't have an agent and you let your publisher sell these rights on your behalf, it's not unusual for the publishers to give the author much less than 85% of that deal. And even more importantly, in this case not only you will receive less money, but any income generated through the sale of subsidiary rights will not come straight to you, but will be set against the advance paid to the author (which means that if your book doesn't sell enough copies or generate enough revenue to earn back the advance already paid, you will not see any serial money at all).

Also when your agent manages to keep those sub rights, you benefit not only economically, but you can have a lot more control and a say on what the third party who wishes to acquire those rights does with your work. You won't need the publishers' approval to do as you wish.

As they run a business, any publisher will always try to pay as little as possible for an author's work. On the other hand, the agent's job is to get the author the best possible deal, which means asking the publisher for a better offer or going to another publisher if they think the first publisher is no offering what the book and author deserve. Without an agent the author is likely to have less bargaining power, and not knowing the market or what standard publishing practice is, she/he might end up accepting the first offer made, even if this is not the best one the book could get.

Also bear in mind that the main trade publishers don't accept unsolicited manuscripts, so authors have to go via agents to try and get their work read anyway.

On the other hand, are you sure you need an agent? It depends on you, your experience and above all the kind of books you write. Not all authors need agents, and agents don't tend to deal with certain type of books. You don't if you are writing in specific genres (Mills & Boon romances, erotic novels, etc.), poetry, academic/technical or educational books, or certain type of practical illustrated books. These authors may well approach the relevant publishers direct. But you do, if you are writing books that are genuinely like to sell in large numbers, and likely to interest several trade publishers.

How long does a manuscript take to be looked at? And how quickly would an author be expecting to hear a reply?

It depends on the agency, the author (if already published or not) and the type of book; and whether your submission is suitable for that particular agency (we regularly get sent children's books, even if all directories specify we don't handle this type of books! So that's a fast 'no, thank you'). It also depends on the time of the year, as certain times tend to be busier than others (for example April for the London Book Fair or October for the Frankfurt Book Fair; or Christmas).

I think it's reasonable to wait at least one month before chasing the agency (unless there are valid reasons for doing so, like for example if you have received some interest elsewhere). However, before sending out your submission, it would be wise to enquire whether that agency is looking for new material – you can save yourself a lot of time, money and effort this way.

In general we tend to acknowledge submissions giving the author an indication of the turnaround time for consideration.

Do you advise writers to approach you once their book is finished or during the course of the creative process?

It depends on the type of book and how experienced an author is. If you are writing your first novel, you'd be advised not only to complete it, but to revise your first draft as many times as necessary before submitting it. Why? Because by the time you finish your book, you might well go back to the beginning and change it considerably, and you don't want to spoil your chances by sending out half-baked material. Few authors are naturally talented, most will need to learn their craft, and practice and revise their work going through a number of edits before they feel it stands a realistic chance of being accepted.

On the other hand, if you are a published author, you could approach an agent with a partial of your next novel to get an initial reaction. This is because having had a book published means you can actually write and have a proven track record of being able to complete it and to the same standard as your initial chapters.

When it comes to non-fiction it is different. You can sell your work to a publisher on the basis of a strong proposal and a couple of good complete chapters. We represent many journalists, and the vast majority of their non-fiction books have been sold on this kind of limited material.

And what should you write in a covering letter?

Remember that agents make up their mind fairly quickly when considering your work, so make sure your work stands out and makes an impact straight away. The covering letter is extremely important: make it brief intriguing clear; the purpose is to present yourself and your work in a professional way and whet the agent's appetite for your work. It shouldn't be longer than one page and certainly not longer than two. You'd need to include anything that would help me to understand and want to represent your book, and help me to sell to a publisher. What should go in? Information on who you are, why you are writing, what you are writing, why will people want to read it, what are your expectations or hopes for your writing, your experience, possible competition for the book, etc.

How much do agents charge? Should an agent charge a reading fee?

Most agents tend to charge 15% (20% for foreign sales or film/TV rights) of the gross amounts received for any deal they negotiate on behalf of their authors. I think only a handful of agents are still charging 10% (and usually to clients they started representing a long time ago).

Agents shouldn't charge any reading fees. Agents should make authors money, not make them pay money for something that should be a normal part of the agent's job like assessing a book. Also the Agents' Association forbids his members from doing so (we belong to it).

However, authors should be reasonable and understand agents can only give detailed comments if they are sufficiently interested in a book, as it's impossible to give feedback to everyone who writes in or the agent wouldn't have time for anything else! Editorial services agencies and literary consultancies charge reading fees – you pay for their editorial report on your book. You pay the agent for getting you deals (and preparing your material for submission is part of the process).

Where is the best place to find an agent? And is it okay to contact more than one at a time?

There are various writers' directories listing agents, their preferences and submission guidelines; and the internet is an invaluable source of information about what the various agents do or like. Or you can try and get one via personal recommendation, by attending events or courses where agents take part, by networking at literary events or similar. I don't think there is anything wrong with contacting more than one agent at a time. However, it would be appropriate to state this fact in your letter. Bear in mind, some agents don't accept submissions unless on an exclusive basis.

What do you look for from a new writer?

It is important for authors to understand that we run a business. Unlike other professionals, agents are paid on results (even if we have done a lot of work on a book, if we don't sell it, we don't make any money), so they have to be cautious about what they take on (that's why it might seem easier to get a publisher than an agent sometimes!).

My criteria for taking someone on are talent, saleability, a professional attitude and hopefully someone willing and capable of a career in writing.

For fiction you want someone who could write ideally a book a year (especially if commercial), so you can build them up with readers. For non-fiction it's fine to have one-offs (for example an autobiography).

I deal with for both mainstream fiction and non-fiction projects. I am looking for originality and what appeals to me personally (topics, themes, etc.) However, the bottom line has to be something that I know I can sell - there is no point in me taking on an author if I don't think a publisher would make an offer, or that thousands of people are going to go and buy it.

When I say original, I don't mean experimental or weird (like typing a few words on a blank page, or writing continuously without punctuation – believe me it has happened!). What I mean is either come up with what hasn't been done before (hard) or give a new unusual twist to something that has proved to be successful. For example, one of the very first authors I took on as an agent was first time novelist Nisha Minhas. She writes amusing and witty romantic comedies with an Asian angle, themes and characters. When I first read her submission we were in an open plan office, and I was so engrossed and was giggling so much that my colleagues stopped working and asked me what I was reading! I realised that I must have been on to something … but why was she original and successful? This was the year 2000, Bridget Jones-mania was still sweeping the country and the first new chick lit authors where proving hugely successful. At the same time 'Goodness Gracious Me' on TV and 'Bhaji on the Beach' at cinemas were showing how popular all things Asian could be in the mainstream; and Arundhati Roy was winning prizes. Enter Nisha: an avid reader, she was writing the kind of book she would have loved to read herself (about British Asian women and their everyday life); and even more importantly, what she was writing fitted in perfectly with where the book market was going, hence the quick (and lovely) first offer from Simon and Schuster only days after we submitted her first novel.

I guess when it comes to fiction; I like strong memorable characters, an original storyline or setting, an international flavour, something not too traditional or cosy. It's hard to define I'm afraid, but it's quite easy to spot it when it is presented in front of you.

I am particularly keen and have been successful with first novelists, journalists, multicultural writing and books about Italy. Most of my authors were actually first time writers when we started working together.

What's the single, most important piece of advice you would give to someone who is looking for an agent?

Write a great book (not just a book) and look for the best possible agent for it – the best agent will be someone who is passionate about your work and someone you are happy to work with at a personal and business level. You'll need to do a fair bit of research on agents, find out what kind of books they represent (this is a great way of working out what they are interested in and have been successful with) and what they are looking for. Make your submission personal to that agent and show you have a reasonable understanding of the market.

So if you are a talented writer, don't give up even if you have received some rejections (but pay attention to what they say and try to work out why it is so, act on constructive criticism), use every setback to spur you to greater effort, persevere, learn more about your craft and the way the publishing industry works. And if you do all this, there is no reason why you shouldn't get yourself a good agent and a book deal!

Last but not least, what is every agents pet hates?

Ah, that's impossible to answer; you'd have to ask each agent. You'll find that agents are very different in style, approach and personality (that's why it's important to find the right one for you and your work). But I guess we find irritating new authors who make extravagant or exaggerated claims about their work in their letters, or who haven't done any basic research about the agency or the type of book they are writing. If you want to make money and a career as an author, you should know it's not a hobby, and that hard work and professionalism are a must.

I guess my personal pet hates would include submissions by authors who have no idea about what I do (and send me science-fiction books for example!), the kind of authors I represent, or authors who spell my name wrong (I'm sure I share this with other people who have 'unusual' or 'interesting' names) …

Passionate about people and books, **Lorella Belli** studied languages and literature at the University of Venice and has worked in publishing since 1996. She set up LBLA Ltd in London's Notting Hill in 2002 and represents bestselling, award-winning, self-published and debut authors and clients worldwide (fiction, non-fiction; both commercial and literary). The agency also handles UK rights on behalf of US and foreign literary agencies, and thanks to its broad international reach, are very successful at selling translation rights on behalf of publishers and other literary agencies, as well as our own authors. We work with co-agents in the USA and worldwide, as well as with film/TV agents, to ensure our writers are represented in all media and territories.

We are particularly proud to represent authors from many different countries and are interested in books with a multi-cultural perspective and a genuine potential to sell well in the UK and internationally.

ABOUT THE INTERVIEWEES

Mohsin Hamid writes regularly for The New York Times, the Guardian and the New York Review of Books, and is the author of *The Reluctant Fundamentalist, Moth Smoke, How to Get Filthy Rich in Rising Asia* and *Discontent* and its Civilisations. Born and mostly raised in Lahore, he has since lived between Lahore, London and New York. His novel, *Exit West,* was shortlisted for the 2017 Man Booker Prize.

Roopa Farooki was born in Lahore in Pakistan and brought up in London. She graduated from New College, Oxford and worked in advertising before turning to write fiction. Roopa now lives in south-east England and south-west France with her husband, twin baby girls and two sons. Bitter Sweets, her first novel, was nominated for the Orange Award for New Writers 2007. Roopa's novels have been published internationally and translated into a dozen languages.

Imran Ahmad was born in Pakistan, grew up in London, and went to Stirling University, before a corporate career that took him all over the world, including five years living in the United States. *Unimagined* is Imran's first book.

Priya Basil was born in London and grew up in Kenya. She now lives in London and Berlin. Her first novel, *Ishq and Mushq*, was shortlisted for a Commonwealth Writer's Prize, and longlisted for the Dylan Thomas Prize and the IMPAC Dublin Literary Award. Priya's novella, Strangers on the 16:02, was one of the annual ten Quick Reads published in

February 2011. In 2010 Priya co-founded Authors for Peace.

Nikita Lalwani was born in Rajasthan and raised in Cardiff. *Gifted* is her first novel and was longlisted for the Man Booker Prize and shortlisted for the Costa First Novel Award and the Glen Dimplex Fiction Award 2007. She lives in London.

Rana Dasgupta won the 2010 Commonwealth Writers' Prize for Best Book for his debut novel *Solo*. He is also the author of a collection of urban folktales, *Tokyo Cancelled*, which was shortlisted for the 2005 John Llewellyn Rhys Prize. *Capital,* his first work of non-fiction, has been shortlisted for The Orwell Prize 2015. Born in Canterbury in 1971, he now lives in Delhi.

Nikesh Shukla is a writer and social commentator. His debut novel, *Coconut Unlimited,* was shortlisted for the Costa First Novel Award 2010 and longlisted for the Desmond Elliott Prize 2011, and his second novel, *Meatspace*, was critically acclaimed. He is the editor of the essay collection, *The Good Immigrant,* where 21 British writers of colour discuss race and immigration in the UK.

H.M. Naqvi has worked in the financial services industry, run a slam venue, and taught creative writing at Boston University. He has received the DSC Prize for South Asian Literature and the Phelam Prize for poetry. Ensconced in Karachi, H.M. Naqvi is working on his second novel.

Roshi Fernando was born in London of Sri Lankan parents. She has a PhD in Creative Writing from the University of Swansea. She won the 2009 Impress Prize, was shortlisted for the 2011 Sunday Times EFG Private Bank Award, longlisted for the 2011 Frank O'Connor International Short Story Prize. Roshi Fernando lives in Gloucestershire with her husband and four children.

Prajwal Parajuly - the son of an Indian father and a Nepalese mother - divides his time between New York and Oxford, England, but disappears to Gangtok, his hometown in the Indian Himalayas, at every opportunity. Parts of *The Gurkha's Daughter: Stories* were written while he was a writer-in-residence at Truman State University, in Kirksville, Missouri.

Rishi Dastidar was educated at Mansfield College, Oxford University and the London School of Economics. His poetry has been published by the *Financial Times,* Tate Modern and the Southbank Centre amongst many others, and has featured in the anthologies *Adventures in Form* and *Ten: The New Wave* (Bloodaxe). A fellow of The Complete Works, he is a consulting editor at *The Rialto* magazine, a member of the Malika's Poetry Kitchen collective, and also serves as a chair of Spread The Word.

Sunjeev Sahota was born in 1981 in Derbyshire and continues to live in the area. *Ours are the Streets* was his first novel and his second, *The Year of the Runaways*, was shortlisted for the 2015 Man Booker Prize and was awarded a European Union Prize for Literature in 2017.

Abir Mukherjee grew up in the west of Scotland. His debut novel, *A Rising Man* won the Harvill Secker/Daily Telegraph crime writing competition and became the first in a series. It went on to win the CWA Historical Dagger and was shortlisted for the Theakstons Old Peculier Crime Novel of the Year award. Abir lives in London with his wife and two sons.

Kamila Shamsie is the author of six novels: *In the City by the Sea*, *Salt and Saffron*; *Kartography*, *Broken Verses*; *Burnt Shadows*, and *A God in Every Stone*, which was shortlisted for the Baileys Prize, the Walter Scott Prize for Historical Fiction and the DSC Prize for South Asian Literature. *Home Fire* was longlisted for the Man Booker Prize 2017, shortlisted for the Costa Best Novel Award, and won the Women's Prize for Fiction 2018. Kamila Shamsie is a Fellow of the Royal Society of Literature and was named a *Granta* Best of Young British Novelist in 2013. She grew up in Karachi and now lives in London.

Meena Kandasamy is a poet, fiction writer, translator and activist who is based in Chennai, Tamil Nadu, India. She has published two collections of poetry, *Touch* (2006) and *Ms. Militancy* (2010). She holds a PhD in socio-linguistics from Anna University Chennai, has represented India at the University of Iowa's International Writing Program and was made the Charles Wallace India Trust Fellow at the University of Kent, Canterbury. *The Gypsy Goddess* is her first novel. Her second novel, When I Hit You was shortlisted for the Women's Prize.

ABOUT THE ASIAN WRITER

The Asian Writer is the voice of British Asian writing and is for readers and writers interested in South Asian literature. It is both the online magazine and quarterly newsletter. It aims to provide a platform for new and emerging writers of South Asian origin as well as showcase their work.

The Asian Writer offers readers an eclectic approach to South Asian writing through profile interviews, Q&A's, and reviews. It features the latest news, original comment and thoughts on contemporary South Asian literature and publishing as well as practical advice and inspiration.

Our objectives are to:

- raise the profile of Asian writers and their works
- discover the best emerging talents and develop their writing skills
- encourage and inspire writers and nourish creativity
- champion diversity in publishing
- publish new writing by British Asian writers

Read more online at http://www.theasianwriter.co.uk

ABOUT THE EDITOR

Farhana Shaikh is a writer and publisher born in Leicester. She is the founding editor of The Asian Writer, an online magazine championing Asian literature. She established Dahlia Publishing to publish regional and diverse writing and the Leicester Writes Festival to celebrate local writing talent. She has facilitated creative writing workshops and judged competitions in the UK and India. She is currently part of Curve Theatre's Cultural Leadership Programme.

In 2010, Farhana received an arts bursary from the Royal Shakespeare Company. She writes feature articles, reviews, poetry and fiction. Her work has featured in *The Independent*, Southbank Centre, Afridiziak and Reviews Hub.

In 2017 she won the Penguin/Travelex Next Great Travel Writer competition. More recently she has been longlisted for the Thresholds International Short Fiction Feature Writing Competition and the Spread the Word Life Writing Prize.

Farhana lives in Leicester but can be found on Twitter talking about books and publishing @farhanashaikh.